THE DIVINING MIND

THE
DIVINING
MIND

A GUIDE TO DOWSING AND SELF-AWARENESS

T. EDWARD ROSS
and RICHARD D. WRIGHT

Illustrated by Robin Rothman

Destiny Books
Rochester Vermont

Destiny Books
One Park Street
Rochester, Vermont 05767

LIBRARY OF CONGRESS CATALOGING–IN–PUBLICATION DATA
Ross, T. Edward.
    The divining mind : a guide to dowsing and self-awareness
/ T. Edward Ross and Richard D. Wright.
       p. cm.
    Includes bibliographical references.
    ISBN 0-89281-263-X
    1. Divining-rod. I. Wright, Richard D., 1933– . II. Title.
BF1628.R68 1989
133.3'23--dc20   89-17192
                                               CIP

Printed and bound in the United States

10 9 8 7 6 5 4 3 2

Destiny Books is a division of Inner Traditions International, Ltd.

Distributed to the book trade in the United States by American International Distribution Corporation (AIDC), Colchester, Vermont.

Distributed to the book trade in Canada by Book Center, Inc., Montreal, Quebec.

Grateful acknowledgement is given to the authors and publishers listed below for permission to reprint excerpts from the following:

    The Mystic Spiral by Jill Purce (London: Thames and Hudson, 1974).

    The Divining Hand by Christopher Bird (New York, E.P. Dutton, 1979).

Contents

Prologue   1

Introduction   5

Part I   Practical Dowsing   9
   1. Basic Tools: The L-Rod   11
   2. A Few Seed Ideas   21
   3. Basic Tools: The Y-Rod   26
   4. Basic Tools: The Pendulum   31
   5. On-Site Dowsing   39

Part II   Grounding the Divining Process   47
   6. Historical Perspective   49
   7. Toward a Dowsing Paradigm   54
   8. The American Society of Dowsers   66

Part III Advanced Concepts in Dowsing   71
   9. The Next Step   73
   10. Map Dowsing   77
   11. The Paradigm and Beyond   87
   12. Dowsing and Healing   103

Epilogue   109

Appendices   113
   Appendix A. Tools for Dowsing   115
   Appendix B. Record Keeping   119
   Appendix C. Completed Map of Site B   121
   Appendix D. Completed Map of Site C   122
   Appendix E. Experimental Accounts   123
   Appendix F. Selected Bibliography   128

To all our teachers, known and unknown.

Prologue

The time is 8:45 a.m. on a Tuesday in mid-September, and low clouds pass rapidly over the hilltop village of Danville, Vermont. Through breaks in the clouds the sun shines intermittently across the village green and onto the plain white front of the Methodist Church. Inside the silent church, spots of color from the stained glass flicker across the backs of the pews, which will soon be filled to capacity with dowsing students. Extra folded chairs lean against the edges of pews and against the wall.

On the other side of the village green, downstairs in the Masonic Hall, several groups of students finish their breakfasts and then stroll outside, clothed for the early morning chill. If the weather reports are correct, the day will be dry but brisk. Cars bearing license plates from all over the United States are parked solidly around the green. By 8:59 a.m. all the students have sorted themselves out to assigned seats in the church. The pews are full. An overflow of students occupy chairs placed against the rear wall. Field instructors sit in folding chairs along the aisles at vantage points from which they can oversee the progress of the men and women who are to be their pupils for the next two days.

At the front of the church the two school directors check last-minute revisions in the script and note changes in the schedule. The clock in the nearby town hall strikes nine, and they take their places behind the two pulpits. "Good morning," one of them says, "and welcome to the annual dowsing school of the American Society of Dowsers. . . ."

That moment signals the beginning, and for the next thirty-six hours the students live, breathe, and even dream dowsing. By the time they complete the school, they know that they have become, not experienced dowsers, but accomplished beginners in an undertaking that has the capacity to change their lives.

The authors of this book supervised the above procedure for four consecutive years, 1984–1987, during which they codirected a series of dowsing schools that introduced and developed a new approach to dowsing. It was one that allowed the students to develop their skills in a practical way, which they expected, but it also led them beyond limitations they might have previously assumed. Most of the students did not realize that it was a new approach, simply because they had never known any other one.

In this approach students were required to create and visualize first the *idea* of the target in their own minds before starting their dowsing practice, and then they were taught how to refine that idea gradually through the three preliminary stages of the seven-stage development of dowsing that was a theme and standard of the school (see Chapter 11).

From the first moments of those schools until the final awarding of certificates, the students studied and practiced dowsing as a natural human ability, a natural reach of their minds that, when developed step by step, could be mastered at each stage with simplicity and ease. They gained confidence by working in small groups and investigating actual targets, both on-site and remote, in and near the village of Danville. Their field instructors, experienced as both dowsers and teachers, came, like them, from all sections of the United States. During those chilly September days the teachers took their students to preselected and surveyed property sites and with patience, constant encouragement, and instant feedback from real targets helped them to develop and refine their dowsing skills. Underground utilities, accurately mapped and maintained from Civil War days, became one set of criteria. Previously dowsed wells became another. Practical dowsing thus served as an introduction to dowsing through space and time and to dowsing for abstract and intangible targets.

Equally as important as the in-class instruction and the on-site dowsing practice with their instructors was the development of the particular dowsing attitude or point of view that is also found in this book. This point of view enabled those students in the four schools to advance smoothly through each successive stage of dowsing and it also gave them the know-how to continue that development after they left the school and returned to the everyday world.

Those schools are now history, but this book is based on them, freely adapted for the general reader. When the original school was first being developed, each of the authors wrote separate parts of the script, but by now the material has been revised and enlarged to such an extent that it would be impossible to say where one author leaves off and the other begins. This result is not primarily a how-to book, although we do include training in dowsing. It is not a history, although it does contain information about the development of dowsing. It is, instead, a book about the reach of the mind and the unlimited potential offered to dowsers by that reach, a potential limited only by the limitations in the consciousness of the dowser.

You will see that this book is in part a manual of basic instructions for developing one's dowsing skill step by step independently, with explanation and encouragement at every stage. More important, however, you will see that it is also an introduction to one possible model for a point of view toward dowsing which we feel is critical—not only for the most harmonious development of dowsers, but also to illuminate the *meaning* of dowsing and place it in the context of our day-to-day living.

The schools that preceded this book could not have been brought into being without the assistance and encouragement of many other people. The field instructors assisted willingly and without compensation, some for all four years. The people of Danville allowed the school directors to map their properties and the students to tramp about to dowse those sites. We thank all of these people, and especially the students, who provided the enthusiasm and perspective that teachers in any field value.

We hope that our presentation will allow each of you, the

readers, to become students in an ongoing dowsing school, so that as you read this book, you may also take those first guided steps toward becoming dowsers with the confidence that will allow you, in turn, to teach others to begin their own dowsing journeys.

Once again, we bid you welcome.

T.E.R.
R.D.W.

Introduction

Our ability to dowse is one of our natural talents, just as our ability to use our intuition is natural. These abilities, which may seem strange to those who have not developed them, are no more difficult or mysterious than, say, our ability to walk or communicate or even think. That doesn't mean that we can necessarily recognize these talents and put them to use unaided, but it does mean that they are abilities we already possess and can develop whenever we feel ready. The problem is that most of us were taught to disregard any such abilities or to label their supposed existence as untrustworthy.

As we take you step by step through the basics of dowsing, one of our goals will be to demystify the subject. We will explain that dowsing is one practical, specific means by which you may gain access to your intuition. We will additionally show you that it is a means, or skill, that extends far beyond the limits that most people, including conventional dowsers, ordinarily assign to their intuitive abilities, because the dowsing skill, when properly developed, not only expresses that intuition but gives form to it and enhances it. There are different levels of dowsing, and we will emphasize the naturalness of activity on all these levels, of which the locating of a vein of water on a site is only the first.

Many of us have grown up with certain misconceptions and have been subjected to a cultural training that tells us we must think of "natural" in only very limited contexts, and that anything outside those limits must by definition be unnatural or supernatural. As you will see, this limitation is simply not so. By the time you finish this book, you will begin to understand how to accept dowsing as a natural part of your life.

Each of us not only has a talent for dowsing, but that talent is already developed to some degree, as you will realize once you learn to use the tools. We will show you how it can be further developed within a conceptual framework so that you may extend it to those increasingly subtle levels. Your initial ability to receive a verifiable dowsing response is the first stage, one of the primary ones for this book, just as it would be for any dowsing workshop or class. Once you master that stage, and the other basic ones we develop in this book, you will be ready, if you so wish, to take further steps. Meanwhile, you will be ready and able to use dowsing practically and creatively for your own personal growth, as well as for service to your fellow men and women and all the other beings on this planet. None of this can be done without training and understanding, however, which is why we attempt to provide general suggestions and specific guidelines covering both of these in this book.

No matter what degree of dowsing proficiency any of us has reached, we are all students. Experience shows us that the more we extend the art of dowsing, the greater the realization we gain of how far we still have to go. As you will soon realize, that is what makes dowsing not only fun but satisfying. One challenge begets another. There are *no limits*. No matter how much we may have learned about dowsing, or how proficient we may have become, we know it is only a beginning, and that greater richness and fulfillment lie ahead. When we do progress, we increase our proficiency, which is important, but it is still only part of the picture. We also find that as our proficiency increases, particularly within the context of the system developed in this book, we also bring ourselves into an increasingly broad and subtle state of balance and awareness, both personally and in relation to the world around us. Our continued practice in the skill of dowsing, particularly if it is well focused, helps to enhance that condition.

We invite you to use this book as a guide and strongly recommend that you move step by step through the instructions. That way, you will build your confidence as you progress through each stage. Briefly, we will (1) introduce you to the tools of dowsing, (2) show you how to make a successful start, (3) suggest a way to think about dowsing that will allow you to develop the idea of the target, (4) show you how to check your ability and gain feedback every step of the way, and (5) encourage you to keep your mind open to the possibilities of endless development into the many aspects of dowsing that lie beyond the scope of this book.

After you gain some mastery in the use of the basic dowsing tools, you will begin learning how to work over actual targets, and these will be targets of which you will know both precise location and description. You will chart them so that the all-important feature of confirmation—the breath of life to any dowser—is immediately available to you. You will progress from material targets in the ground (including, if your location permits, the evaluation of a successfully dowsed and drilled site) to exposure to remote dowsing and all that it implies.

Remember, our goal is to guide you through the basics so that you will master those beginning levels and develop the ability and desire to progress to increasingly subtle levels of dowsing when you are ready. The very first time your dowsing instrument responds to a verifiable target, seemingly of its own volition, is as significant as the first tentative steps taken by an infant. Awkward as they may be, they elicit great joy, even though we know that there are many more steps that must be taken before we master the skill of moving forward without stumbling. We will create a paradigm for dowsing that will help you make each of the steps you take a step for growth, because we feel that if a person is to develop dowsing skill to its fullest extent, one must set one's mind to a particular open-ended way of thinking, and must follow a particular sequence of increasingly subtle stages of dowsing.

If you follow the procedures in the sequence that we present them in this book, and if you set your mind to the way of thinking that we feel is appropriate for developing the dowsing potential we all possess, you will have a very good chance of unfolding that ability in a way that will allow you to become, at each level, an accomplished dowser.

PART I

PRACTICAL DOWSING

Be an opener of doors for such as come after thee and do not try to make the Universe a blind alley.

—Ralph Waldo Emerson

What we consider supernatural becomes natural, while that which we have always seen as so natural reveals how wondrously supernatural it is.

—Frederick Franck

1

Basic Tools: The L-Rod

Everyone has the innate ability to become a dowser, and the first step is to obtain a verifiable dowsing response. For most beginners the idea of obtaining a response creates apprehension, but that first step is no more difficult to learn than the skill of hammering a nail without bending it or riding a bicycle without a wobble. These are skills that require practice along with a measure of confidence, but whether the skill is hammering or bicycling or dowsing, a conscientious student can catch on rapidly and develop a level of confidence that will constantly increase, just as the skill does.

ASKING THE QUESTION

We'll begin with a simple comparison. As you set out to master the preliminary stages of dowsing, think of your brain as being in part like a computer, perhaps a supercomputer, that essentially operates from a series of on–off synapses. The dowsing that you do with the standard dowsing tools is also essentially an on–off process. The tool produces a binary readout, a "yes" or "no" answer. Let's say that you are ready to dowse a site. You hold your L-rods in your hands as in Figure 1 and ask, is there water here? If there is water there, and if you have trained yourself properly, the rods swing out as in Figure 2, indicating "yes." Like a child's game, one phrases the question so that it can be answered in a binary fashion, with a "yes" or a "no." That is the first point. It is a simple one, but it is also a vitally important one. There must be a clearly defined and observable indication of "yes" and of "no." The second point is that in any search, whether that search is on-site or remote, one proceeds

Figure 1. The dowser holds the L-rods like two pistols, parallel to the ground, in the search position.

from the yes–no questions that are more general to those that are increasingly more specific. Let's say we are on a site and have found our target. Now we ask, is there a water pipe beneath this lawn? Yes. Am I over it? Yes. Is it one, two, three feet deep? Yes, at three feet. Is it copper? No. Is it iron? Yes. Is its diameter half-inch? . . . and so on. One specific question, one specific answer, beginning with the whole or general picture and then narrowing down to the more particular. You will find it helpful to hold the following concept in mind: *the answer is in the question, and learning to dowse is learning to ask the right questions.*

A CONCEPT OF WATER

Now you are ready to begin. Your first target will be right in front of you, and it will be connected with water, the target most people associate with dowsing. Before that, however, we will set the scene by illustrating how a dowser thinks of water. Unlike many conventional hydrologists and well drillers, a dowser is concerned with underground flowing water. That's what he seeks, and that's what he finds. Often he finds it right beside a dry hole that's already been drilled, and he finds it at less depth, and with good volume, too. He sometimes finds it where a conventional scientist says it shouldn't exist, a verifiable fact that causes some scientists to feel very uneasy. That explains why dowsers soon learn to be very diplomatic with hydrologists or with the well driller who drilled into a water table that wasn't there.

Unlike the conventional scientist, the dowser conceives of a font, or rise, of water emanating from very deep in the earth (Figure 3). He sees it thousands of feet down, where it seems to him to be continually forming under conditions of great heat and pressure, rising in a column through orifices in the crust, perhaps in a series of sideways moves, until it either runs out of pressure or strikes something quite impenetrable. It then makes a 90-degree turn and, generally following the contours of the surface, heads for the nearest stream, lake, or ocean, very much like streams of water would do on the surface of the ground. These underground "veins," as Leonardo da Vinci likened them, come in all sizes. Perhaps you have felt the colder flow

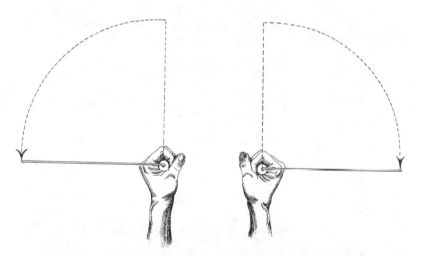

Figure 2. The L-rods open outward to indicate a positive, or "yes," response. If the answer were negative, or "no," the rods would remain as in Fig. 1.

coming up through the sand in the warm ocean off Miami, or had a drink from the Castalian Spring surging out of the limestone heights of Mt. Parnassus at Delphi. These veins of water flow everywhere, and these are the veins we mean. They are the ones a dowser trains himself to respond to, before they surface from underground, in his search for water.

If we were in Key Biscayne or at Delphi, we could easily show you how your L-rods would swing in your hands as you crossed these sites. But we can also tell you how to do it right now from wherever you are.

RESPONDING TO THE IMAGE

Now we'll explain how you may set up your first target. Remember, we said this was like a child's game. It is based on the *idea of water*, an idea that we all carry with us whether we realize it or not. As you know, we are continually involved with water, and this involvement is so essential that we have, enfolded within our minds, all the information we need to create an image of water at will.

Your first step will be to obtain a response to the image that you create. To do this you first focus your attention on the edge of your table or the back of a chair, and you imagine that it indicates the location of a stream of water that is flowing, deep out of sight, directly underneath it. You now concentrate on this *idea*, or image, not of the object in front of you, but of this imagined underground stream of water flowing beneath the edge of that table or desk or chair back that you are facing. And don't let yourself be intimidated by that phrase "idea of water"; simply imagine that your target is a stream of flowing water, and make that image as vivid as you can.

Next hold the L-rods in your hands as though they are two pistols (see Figure 1). As you see, the L-rods are nothing more

Figure 3. Water emanating from deep within the earth rises under pressure to form domes, or pockets of water, which spread outward in underground streams, or veins. These veins may reach the surface as pure spring water or may be the source of pure water for a well.

than lengths of metal rod, bent at right angles, with sleeves of plastic or other material for the grips. (Appendix A contains directions for making the basic dowsing tools.) Make sure that they are able to swing freely without their touching your hands. The rods should be held so that they are parallel to each other and as level as you can keep them without their wobbling. You may want to walk around with them for a while until you can easily keep them straight and parallel. Also, make sure that your shoulders and arms are relaxed, just as they had to be when you first rode a bicycle.

Now stand near the edge of the table or desk or chair with the L-rods pointed forward and imagine that flowing stream of water. Lean or walk forward with your L-rods balanced straight and parallel. As you do so, remember to keep your mind focused on the *idea of water*, on that vivid image of a stream. Then, as you pass over the near edge of the flow you have imagined, the L-rods should open outward. If they do not do so at first, don't worry. You're asking yourself to accept a response that is new, so you may have to take a few moments to practice consciously making the rods open by moving your wrists slightly. As you do open them, remind yourself that this is the response you seek. Then you should repeat the process until the L-rods consistently open outward, seemingly of their own volition, with no physical effort on your part, at the point at which you have imagined the stream of flowing water.

Next you notice whether the reaction occurs as the tips of your rods cross over the "stream" or as your hands do. Both are valid responses, and you should practice with your imagined target until you can receive a response either way. Later on you will find that there are times when one indication is more appropriate to your purpose than the other. One of the two reactions will seem to be the more natural one for you, and you should make note of this choice. In the future, when you are working outside on actual targets, you will want to locate things accurately and know whether your response is in relation to the movement of your rods, your body, your hands, or even your feet.

You have now practiced with your L-rods so that they open when you reach the *near* edge of your target. If you continue

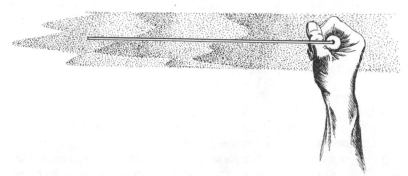

Figure 4. The L-rod points in the direction toward which the water is flowing.

moving forward with the rods open until you pass the *far* edge of your target, they will return to their parallel position. Practice approaching and passing this imagined stream until the opening and closing of the rods becomes automatic, for both of these indications will be important when you are doing on-site work later and have to determine the depth and size of an underground stream of water.

Next you will determine one particular characteristic of your imagined stream, the direction in which it is flowing. To do this you take one of the rods in your dominant hand (right if you are right-handed, left if left-handed) and approach your target as you did before, this time telling yourself that you want the rod to point downstream, as in Figure 4. Your rod should begin to turn as you approach the stream and then follow the flow when you are over it. If you approach the stream from a slightly different angle, the rod should still swivel so that it remains pointed toward the direction of flow, much as it would if it were actually immersed in flowing water. Remember that at this stage you are practicing on *the idea of a stream.* You are creating that idea within your own mind and transferring it to the space before you.

The reason that we have adopted this mode will become increasingly clear as we move ahead and begin verifying actual targets of all sorts. By the time you reach the end of this book, you will have covered many of the basic dowsing activities in the same manner, and you will have done so easily and with a sense of naturalness, safety, and comfort.

A FEW PRACTICAL DETAILS

Even though most beginners feel a desire to move ahead rapidly and learn everything at once, *the basics come first and must be mastered first*. In this case the basics mean the ability to get consistently accurate responses with the L-rods without your making any conscious movement. That mastery allows you to remain grounded and avoid most of the subsequent pitfalls that beset dowsers at every stage of their development.

After you have thoroughly mastered these first basic dowsing responses with the L-rod, you might add some bits and pieces to the material you have already been given.

Remember that we said to notice where the reaction took place, at the tips of the rods or as your hands (or even your feet) crossed the target. That is the response that is basic for you, but it will be to your advantage to train yourself to be able to receive a response in several ways. There will be times when you will find one of these ways to be more appropriate. For example, if you let the reaction occur at the tips of your L-rods, you allow yourself a little advance notice of where the target is, whether it be a pipe or a narrow vein of water or an electrical cable. In fact, if you consciously program the *tips* to "lock on" to the target, they will continue to move backward as you pass that target.

If, on the other hand, you program the reaction to occur when your *hands* are over the target, you can then line up the target with them as you look down. With this programming, if you then pass beyond the desired point on the target, the rods will return to the search position, which may be what you desire if you are, say, locating both sides of your target. In that case, when you are in the target zone, such as over a large stream of underground water, you keep the image but request that your rods open again as you leave that zone or as you pass its far edge.

This matter of dowsing a precise location on the target becomes important for any target—water or hydrocarbons or minerals or earth energies. In the case of a good-sized water vein,

Figure 5. The dowser programs the response so that the L-rods will open at the center of the vein to show the angle of flow of the vein of water in relation to the dowser. He approaches the target, crosses its edge, and reaches its center.

you will want to seek the exact location on the cross section of the vein where it is best to drill. It may be the center of it or it may be off-center, wherever is the best place to drill. It may even be at a specific point along the vein where the drill will intersect two or more veins flowing horizontally at different depths.

For this work the precision of your question is all-important, and often you must do a little homework before you know what question to ask—what is involved with drilling for water or for oil, how you "open" a mineral vein, and so on. Remember, the more bits of information you can load into the binary computer you carry inside you, the more knowledge you can then put behind a question, and as a result the more precise your answer will be.

We also suggested that you try to determine the direction in which your imagined vein of water would be flowing. If your L-rod turned toward the right, it did so for good psychological reasons, because we are all naturally accustomed to movement from left to right, as in reading this book. If you are aware of that natural tendency, you can erase it when you are in the field and know that you are being neutral. Having the L-rod point in the direction *toward* which the water is flowing, rather than *from* which it is flowing, also makes good sense because, as we said earlier, if you immersed that L-rod in a stream, it would naturally be forced to turn in that direction.

A final advantage of the L-rods is that if you program the response to occur at the tips, you can immediately discover the angle at which you approach your target, no matter whether it be a pipe or electrical wire or water vein. As in Figure 5, the rod that first contacts the target as you approach it from an angle will respond first; both rods will eventually open to show you the angle of the target in relation to you, the dowser.

Your first responsibility, however, is to develop the ability to get a dowsing response easily and naturally. That sense of naturalness is essential, because we want you to experience dowsing as an activity that is utterly normal and everyday, a resource you can call on at any time, for any valid reason, and that will produce results for you in connection with the most practical as well as the most esoteric problems of daily living. We start with water because it's an essential target; we hold that the ability to locate an underground stream or pipe of flowing water while walking directly over it *must* be the first accomplishment for any dowsing student, no matter what his ultimate goal may be. We want dowsing to become a plus in the daily round, based solidly on results that are wholesome and sound, because we know that if it is, the higher good of a raising of consciousness will automatically take place, and in the long run that is what dowsing is all about.

In Chapter 3 we will take up the second basic dowsing tool, the Y-rod. Before that, however, we would like to take a chapter to develop further some seed ideas that we hope will take root, now that you have had some practice with your L-rods.

2

A Few Seed Ideas

In Chapter 1 we stressed ease and naturalness as important states necessary for good dowsing, but it does require effort to maintain these states. If we are not careful, we tend to slide into one or more self-limiting conditions. We may, for example, try to create and then impose systems of unnecessary complexity on the straightforward process of dowsing. It is certainly a complex process, just as walking or speaking is complex, but we learn and use dowsing as a unified process with a single goal in mind, as we did when we learned to walk or speak. Some beginners may also try to use dowsing to create an air of mystery or a special atmosphere about themselves, and their friends may unwittingly encourage them to do so, but the ability to become a good dowser is no more unique or mysterious than the ability to become a good cook or gardener or carpenter. It does require a degree of concentration and imagination, and the willingness to practice in easy stages, but that skill comes with practice.

We can prevent self-limiting conditions, at least to a certain degree, by the way we speak and think about the dowsing response. When we try to tell ourselves about it, we therefore say something like "The rods did this," or "The pendulum says thus-and-so," but we remember all the while that we are using merely a convenient turn of phrase. The dowsing tool certainly has no volition or will of its own, but for our convenience we speak *as though* the rod or the pendulum were doing the work.

There are good reasons for speaking this way. First, to do so helps us avoid the all-too-common problem of snap judgment. Think of the number of times a day we make decisions that are founded less on fact than they are on emotional or self-centered bias. We ask you to exclude these very human and very limiting tendencies from the dowsing act by trusting your dowsing and allowing it to connect you with the truth by itself. If we give in to those demands of our limited bias, we may end up rationalizing them and acting upon them in all sorts of ingenious ways, to the detriment of our dowsing ability. As we develop our dowsing skill, we also develop, with increasing subtlety, the potential to place ourselves in resonance with the external world (and indeed the internal world, too) on a level beyond that of our gross senses and beyond the scheming of our fantasies, and we do so with immediate and verifiable feedback. But our fantasies may still drift back to an attitude of self-aggrandizement. We may then feel a tendency to think "*I* found this," or "*My* dowsing rod tells me . . .," and if we do harbor such thoughts, the fact that dowsing is a natural mode of fact-finding and communication can become lost, its development limited to the narrow and restricting horizons of the limited ego, the little "I."

The process of dowsing, by its very nature, will help us to develop our awareness and avoid the ego-centered attitudes that curtail personal growth. Whenever we consciously use dowsing as a process by which we may develop stages of awareness *beyond* our ordinary limited concept of self, rather than as a process to enhance that limited concept, we have a better chance to avoid those self-limiting attitudes. The only limits that any of us have to the potential reach of dowsing are those that we put there ourselves. If we can break away from the false constructs that we have allowed to become the mental habits with which we surround ourselves, we can eventually become in phase with an infinitely larger, more dynamic concept of ourselves. One way we may do so is by means of that little bit of metal and plastic we use as a dowsing device. When we establish the convention that it is the device, rather than our personal selves, that is giving the answers, we have a greater opportunity to bypass the little "I" and receive our answers with more confidence and assurance that they are authentic.

Furthermore, when we do hold this idea that it is the device that is responsible for the answers, we also bypass the rational mode of our brain and receive answers channeled a bit more directly through the intuitive mode, which is the mode related more directly to creativity and holistic awareness. We do not suggest that we should throw out the rational mode and adopt only the intuitive, but we do need to give the intuitive greater attention. After all, we have been raised and trained in a society that says the rational, logical approach is the *only* valid approach on which to base our lives and our interaction with the world in which we live. So until we get used to deemphasizing the rational and bringing it into a proper balance with the intuitive, we have to use indirection so that our responses move away from that strictly rational mode. Acting as though the dowsing device were getting the answers is one way of providing that indirection and allowing ourselves to use a greater portion of our intuitive talent.

When we speak of dowsing, we refer to it as a *process*, by which we mean that it sets up conditions for the gradual unfolding of our stages of awareness. We use this manner of speaking because of still another factor that becomes increasingly important as we intensify our internal relationship to our external world. That factor is our nervous system, which, in some respects, is rather similar to an antenna system. If this biological antenna that is part of us were laid out cell by cell, it would stretch out to approximately 27 miles. Through this gigantic antenna we constantly pick up all sorts of information from our environment on all sorts of levels of subtlety, and for our own good our biological systems censor nearly all of it. You can imagine what a state we would be in if this censoring did not take place. All this incoming information becomes part of the tremendously complex and chaotic interplay that goes on continually among the cells, so that the small portion not censored provides the basis for us to construct a basically adequate *concept* of the world around us, which then allows us to function in a seemingly rational manner. We thus build and maintain a conservative image of a world we think we can safely deal with, accepting only the information that will verify our preconceptions. This image then defines our basic stage of awareness.

In opposition to such lifetime habits of thought, our intent when we learn to dowse must be to remove a critical few of the censors, just enough at each successive stage to persuade our biosystem to relay a message to move a device in a predetermined manner so that we can get an appropriate, verifiable response to a specific question, thought, or idea. In order to prevent error as we develop our ability to dowse naturally and easily, we must use patience. We must first learn and then master each stage thoroughly before we try to move on to the next appropriate stage.

In order to teach you how to use the various dowsing devices quickly and with confidence, we are asking you to begin your training by playing what may seem like a game of make-believe. As you read these preliminary chapters and practice the exercises that help you develop the idea of the target, you can be fairly certain that there is not *really* any vein of water under the edge of your table or the back of your chair. However, when you create that image of a vein of water, you are setting up the request to yourself that your system react *as though* there were in fact a vein of water there. If the request succeeds, you are then able to practice the standard dowsing response.

Your biosystem already knows how to attune itself to and handle these ideas, if you let it. After all, you have walked over veins of water thousands of times in your lifetime, mentally ignorant of and unaffected by them, yet every single time that antenna system of yours has picked up all the information about them and their effects on you, sometimes alerting you to their destabilizing effect—perhaps with an arthritic twinge or a headache or some other bodily reaction.

This information, along with a staggering amount of other information, has already been received and encoded within your brain, even though the brain has censored it from your everyday awareness. Experiments pioneered by neurophysiologist Karl Pribram have indicated that much of this information is encoded in a holographic manner throughout the brain. This seemingly innocuous indication has a far-reaching implication. If it is indeed so, this suggests that any item of information resonating across the interstices of the brain is potentially in contact with all other items of information so stored, interacting with them and being affected by them.

This encoding is no small matter, either. In a portion of our neocortex no larger than the size of a pinhead, there are between 30,000 and 100,000 neurons; within that pinhead portion those neurons are joined by about a mile of axons. The encoding is beyond our comprehension, but even so, it is only a small part of the whole. Beyond that inconceivable complexity of encoding that exists within our brains, there lies an even greater and more subtle encoding theorized to exist outside that biological mechanism. In *A New Science of Life* (London, Blond and Briggs, 1981), biologist Rupert Sheldrake suggests that our brains lie within a larger field, which is the field of our minds, and that within our minds we have access potentially to material beyond even those rich complexities of our isolated brains—if we can train ourselves to establish the appropriate resonance with it.

Furthermore, this line of thought suggests (as we will explain in a later chapter) that if we create the appropriate resonance through our thoughts and images, we can then make contact with an even greater holographic-like reality which lies not only beyond our usual concept of ourselves, but even beyond our conventional understanding of the nature of reality itself.

We will offer additional comments about these concepts after you have been introduced to the other basic tools. At the moment it is sufficient to realize that it is all there, all the information you need, within yourself. As you progress to each stage of dowsing, you will develop the ability to unfold it, but only as appropriate, accepting the limitations of each new stage and gently mastering them. Your goal, as you practice using the dowsing tools, is to remove with safety a few of those censors with which our systems have been equipped and to let the appropriate information come through by a simple, threefold process: (1) asking a precise question, (2) creating a precise resonance, and (3) obtaining precise results.

3

Basic Tools: The Y-Rod

If, as we suggest, you progress step by step through this book, you will have practiced enough with the L-rods so that they will respond with consistent accuracy to a target that you have created. You have also studied a few concepts that we will enlarge upon and develop later, after you have had exposure to and practice with the basic tools.

The next device with which you will work is the Y-rod, the instrument most people associate with dowsing. It is a more traditional instrument than the L-rods, but you may find it somewhat more difficult to master. Most people have at least seen pictures of an old-time dowser using a forked stick made from a willow or an apple branch. Ancient woodcuts show the European miner using just such devices. Those devices work well, but their modern equivalent is usually made of plastic (see Appendix A). No matter what the device is made of, there are two characteristics that all Y-rods have in common: they are somewhat springy, and they are hard to break. That latter characteristic is important because you hold the Y-rod so that it is in a state of tension. This puts some strain on it as well as on yourself.

Many dowsers prefer to use the Y-rod rather than the L-rod if they are working on-site in the field or woods. They find that it is easier to use than an L-rod if there is strong wind, because it will not be deflected as an L-rod will. They also find it easier to use over rough terrain, where it is held firmly to prevent it from wobbling. The extra physical effort needed to hold it this way also helps the dowser to remain focused clearly on the target. With experience, that first gentle tug of the Y-rod can be readily felt, and the degree of its strength can relay to the dowser shadings of information that may not be obtained with an L-rod.

HOLDING THE Y-ROD

Your first step is to learn to hold the Y-rod correctly. Begin by holding both hands out, palms up. Place one fork, or branch, of

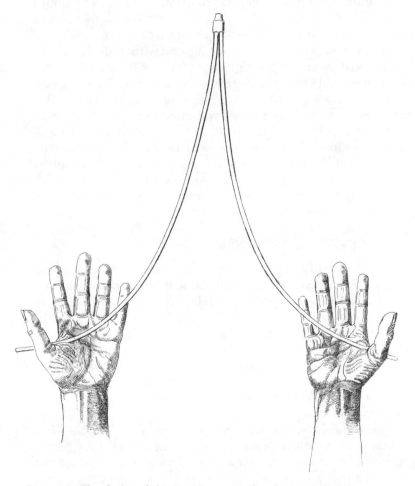

Figure 6. The forks of the Y-rod rest in the dowser's hand.

the Y-rod in each hand, as in Figure 6. Then close your hands securely and firmly over the two ends. Next, hold the Y-rod so that it points outward and upward at about 45 degrees. Adjust the lateral bend of each branch, or fork, of the rod and the twist of each wrist so that you can put tension on it and barely hold it in place (see Figure 7). Hold it in this state of tension just tightly enough to avoid its springing either downward or upward. While maintaining this search position, you should remain relaxed as you walk around, without feeling as though you have to tiptoe to keep the rod from snapping up or down.

After you have practiced walking around with it, the next step is to become aware of the different "feel" of it when you approach your target and it begins to dip. This feeling is quite subtle, and at first you may not notice its special signals. The tension in your hands and wrists will cause the rod to tremble in a way that you may confuse with an authentic tug. Even so, if you hold the idea of the target firmly in mind as you approach it, you will soon begin to notice a definite tug. It is important to become able to identify this tug as soon as possible, so that you do not simply try to compensate for it as you would for an ordinary trembling.

PRACTICING THE RESPONSE

Now you are ready to practice obtaining a response, which you will do in the same way that you did with the L-rod. You hold the Y-rod in the search position while standing near the edge of the desk or the back of the chair. Visualize clearly that stream of water and then step or lean toward the target. The rod will begin to tug, but the feeling may be lost in the general wobble. When you do recognize the tug, allow the rod to follow through. Your rod will dip more and more until, when you finally reach the target, it suddenly completes its dip, sometimes with a snap, and points downward.

Because the response with the Y-rod may at first be more difficult to develop than a comparable response with the L-rod, you may have to use a greater degree of patience. If you are not aware of any tug as you approach and go over the target, then start again; you are simply holding the rod too tightly. The

Figure 7. The dowser holds the Y-rod in the search position.

following procedure will help correct that problem: (1) hold the rod in the search position, (2) reinforce the idea of water, (3) visualize the stream as vividly as possible, and (4) consciously cause the rod to dip in the manner described above. As it moves smoothly downward, tell yourself that this is the response you wish to develop. Once you become accustomed to that tug of the Y-rod, you can then program it to dip without your conscious assistance as it crosses the leading edge of the "stream."

You next practice giving your attention to the far edge of that imaginary stream and receiving a response with your Y-rod when you reach that farther edge. As you hold the rod in the search position and approach the "stream," the rod should pass over the leading edge with *no* response, but it should begin to dip as it approaches that farther edge. It is all a matter of programming, and you have to learn to (1) formulate exactly the right question or image, (2) hold it in your mind, and (3) get precisely the response that you desire.

With practice you will cause the rod to respond exactly to the program or question that you set for it, and that gentle tug will let you know the degree to which you have begun to arrive at your target. It is important for you to remember that you are also training yourself to think and respond in a mode that may be entirely new. Part of you may not particularly want to adjust to the process. You must therefore proceed with the retraining patiently and without frustration.

As you develop your ability to use the Y-rod, you will notice one of the important differences between it and your L-rod: whereas the L-rod may require your sense of sight for feedback and verification, the Y-rod is more responsive to the sense of touch for the same information. You *feel* the rod move; you *feel* it snap down. Your sight can thus be free to guide you over rough terrain or to help you concentrate more fully on the target rather than the device.

As mentioned, many people find the Y-rod more difficult to master than the L-rod, but if you are willing to take the time to develop that "feel" of it and train yourself to recognize that tug, you will soon be able to use it with less and less conscious effort and will be able to act as though the rod alone were doing the work.

4

Basic Tools:
The Pendulum

We now move to the last of the basic dowsing devices, the pendulum. This device is the most popular, potentially the most rewarding, and historically the most misunderstood of all the dowsing tools. More than any other instrument it is the one most commonly associated with unfounded claims. Some treatises speak of the pendulum as if it were a conduit to the spirit world, able to connect us to a source that can give us all sorts of compelling messages from the vasty deep. Other books talk about it as a mysterious device that will lead you to untold riches, romance, and personal fulfillment. Many of these publications do not even use the term *dowsing*. The paradox for us is that the claims, although sensationalized, may indeed contain a germ of truth, but that truth is so distorted by exaggeration, superstition, and appeals to egotism that, if they answer any need at all, it is only to a limited and superficial part of our nature. If you have read such claims, your first task is to recognize their sideshow appeal and disregard them for the moment. You may, in fact, find it helpful to disregard everything you thought you knew about the pendulum and be willing to start with a fresh outlook.

Because of such claims and distortions, we need to remind ourselves that a pendulum, whether it is metallic, crystalline, wooden, or earthen, is simply a balanced weight on the end of a string or chain. Some pendulums have a greater "liveliness" than others and respond with greater alacrity, depending on their shape and mass, but the important factor is that those that work best have a weight at the end that is well centered, as with a plumb bob, so that they can swing freely in all directions without any built-in predisposition or bias. Some people attribute special qualities to pendulums made from various metals or crystals, and you may decide to use something fancy, just as some people may decide to use a fancy hammer or bicycle. Remember, however, that at this stage the only special qualities it may possess are the ones that you give it. For our purposes a hexagonal nut tied to the end of a length of thread will do the job just as well as the most expensive crystalline pendulum.

The primary advantage of all pendulums is that they can be programmed to respond in a large number of ways. This feature can also cause misunderstanding and confusion, because many people use the pendulum without having consciously developed a system for programming it. Some end up believing that the pendulum itself is showing, or "picking up," a degree of mysterious, independent intelligence. This can be a very exciting way to think, but it can also be, at best, a severely limiting presumption. Remember that any response shown by the pendulum comes from you and through you, and that you are the one in charge. To put it another way, if you train yourself correctly, you will program yourself to produce a large number of automatic responses that will cause the pendulum to move in a variety of predetermined patterns so that shades of meaning can be obtained beyond "yes" or "no"—for example, "yes but," "not exactly," "maybe in this one case," "wrong question," and so forth. Unintentional patterns are difficult to translate and may cause confusion, but the confusion is in your own mind, not in the instrument. That's why we recommend that you keep the coding simple at the beginning and remain focused exclusively and exactly on the response you desire.

You'll find yourself giving more attention to the movements of the pendulum than you do to the other dowsing devices, which is all to the good, because then it can act more than the other tools as a biofeedback device. This means that as long as you are willing to train yourself step by step on verifiable targets, you can eventually tune yourself to very subtle and abstract levels of dowsing with results not solely dependent on external factors. It is therefore especially important to be very clear about the questions you ask when you use the pendulum, to release any concepts or assumptions that may limit the reach of your mind, and to remain well versed in the basic uses of this dowsing tool. Otherwise you may mislead yourself into thinking that a verifiable response to a concrete target means that you are ready for any of the more subtle stages. In other words, if you attempt the advanced stages without appropriate training, you may simply get verification of your own misunderstandings.

TUNING THE PENDULUM

Before you begin to use your pendulum, your first task is to "tune" it, which means that you must find the position on the string or chain that will result in the pendulum having a period of swing that is most resonant with your own basic, overall bodily vibration. You do this by holding the string close to the weight at the end of the pendulum, as in Figure 8.

Then you swing the pendulum back and forth as you *slowly* let

Figure 8. The dowser holds the string or chain close to the weight at the end of the pendulum and swings it back and forth as he slowly lets out the string between thumb and index finger.

Figure 9. The pendulum begins to circle clockwise or counterclockwise when it is properly "tuned" to the dowser's vibrational patterns.

out the string with your thumb and index finger. After you have let the string out an inch or two, the pendulum will begin to circle either clockwise or counterclockwise, seemingly without help, as in Figure 9. This is the point at which the pendulum is "tuned" to your present mental rate or "vibratory rate." It is the point at which the pendulum will give a response to your questions most readily. Because a person's vibrational patterns do change from time to time, you should establish the tuning of your pendulum each time you use it. You can still get a response no matter where you hold it, but if it is tuned properly, the response will be instant and definite.

We encourage you to program a simple back-and-forth movement as the search mode because this is the way your pendulum will naturally swing as you approach a target you believe to be ahead of you and beneath the ground. After the pendulum is tuned, you then program it for yes or no. Generally speaking, clockwise is best for "yes" and counterclockwise is best for "no," so you rotate your pendulum clockwise while telling yourself that this motion means "yes," or positive. Then, as you rotate it counterclockwise, you tell yourself that this motion means "no," or negative. Pay no attention at this time to any other movements the pendulum makes; program yourself only for a "yes" or "no" response.

You should practice this programming until the movement becomes second nature. Within a short time you should reach the stage at which you can look at the pendulum when you are moving it in the search mode indicated above, and ask it to indicate "yes," or positive. As you practice, it will move clockwise as if in answer to your request. Likewise, if you ask it to show you "no," or negative, it will move counterclockwise. All that is required is a relaxed state and patience, along with the willingness to act as though the pendulum were responding independently. If nothing happens, go back to moving it consciously and reminding yourself which motions mean "yes" and which ones mean "no." If tension or frustration begin to take over, quit for a while and try again later.

PRACTICING WITH THE PENDULUM

Once the movements become second nature, you may then follow the same procedure that you used when practicing with the L-rod and the Y-rod. First move the pendulum in the search mode (the back-and-forth motion) and walk toward the edge of the table or desk or the back of the chair, holding the *idea* of water again firmly in mind. As you approach the target, which is that stream of water you are presently imagining, the pendulum will begin to move in a clockwise oval; when you are directly over the target, the pendulum will be moving in a circle, as in Figure 10. If you continue beyond the target, the pendulum will begin to move back to an oval and eventually return to back-and-forth, the search mode. You decide the distance that you want to be from the target when the oval motion begins or ends, and then program yourself to communicate that response to the pendulum.

You may notice that when you reach the distance from the

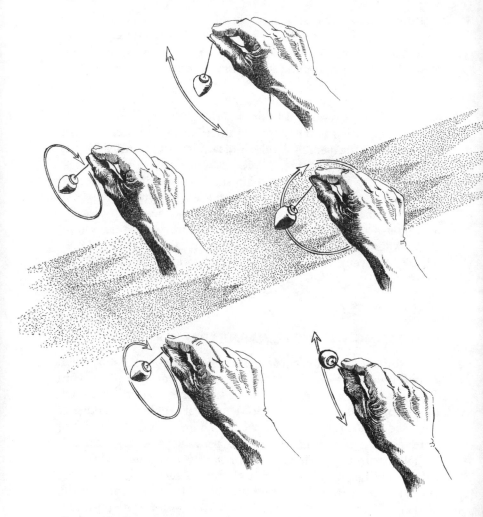

Figure 10. Programmed to circle over the center of a target, the pendulum swings back and forth as the dowser approaches the target. At the leading edge of the target, the pendulum moves into a clockwise oval. It rotates in a full circle over the center of the target. At the outer edge it again moves into an oval, and beyond the target it returns to a swing back and forth.

target that you've programmed, the pendulum forms an oval at about the two o'clock position. That is one example of the kind of subtle response you will produce in the pendulum. In this case two o'clock means "Not yet, but we're almost there." You may cause other responses to become programmed through your subconscious, and this is all right as long as you have first mastered the basics and you, the dowser, remain in charge. However, be wary of random motions at this time. They are no more significant than random thoughts that intrude upon any effort to concentrate. Train yourself to respond only to the target that you seek.

You can also practice the negative, or counterclockwise, motion by holding the idea that the pendulum will indicate "no" whenever you are *not* on target. To do this activate your pendulum in the search mode and ask, for example, "Am I over the center of my stream of water?" Your pendulum should begin to rotate counterclockwise, indicating "no." When you do reach the nearest edge of your target, the pendulum will have gone from counterclockwise, to an oval, back to the search mode, then to a clockwise oval, becoming fully circular when you are over the center of the stream. We repeat, however, that whatever response you develop, *you are the one in control,* so that at this point any other response indicates either a random error or sloppy thinking.

And finally, when you begin to practice, keep in mind that at first you may have to assist the pendulum to change its swing as you approach and pass the target. As you approach it, you create the oval swing and say, "This means that I am now approaching the target." When you reach the target, swing the pendulum in a full circle, saying "This means that I am over the target." You repeat this process until the movement of the pendulum becomes automatic.

If you follow this procedure with a strong image of the target and remind yourself of what the response indicates, then eventually the response will arise automatically. You are, after all, training *yourself* to give an intuitive response, and that training cannot be hurried.

Remember that training the subconscious to use the pendulum is a little like training a high-spirited but well-meaning and intelligent animal. Be kind but firm, allow some leeway, and remember who is in charge. Remember also that the animal, for all its intelligence, may at times be both ornery and mischievous.

5

On-Site Dowsing

By now you have practiced using the three basic dowsing devices. You learned how to develop an accurate response, and you also learned how to focus your mind on the idea, or image, of the target, in this case the *idea* of an underground flowing stream of water. Your next step will be to continue to practice these two processes you have learned by doing them on an actual site with a known target. The principle will be exactly the same: you will put the dowsing tool in the search mode, determine exactly what it is that you want to find, visualize it clearly, and start the search. The only difference is that you will determine your targets through a series of questions that will proceed from the general to the specific and will elicit increasingly detailed responses. We are developing not subtlety but specificity, because at this stage we are still working at the more elementary levels of dowsing and are simply learning to develop the binary, or yes–no, process of dowsing. Remember that although any dowsing activity may still seem new to you, it involves an internal process that is natural to you. You will continue to practice applying your skill and developing your ability to ask questions so that you will, in time, be able to obtain an accurate response that is determined by and limited to the particular question you ask or target you seek.

Before you begin this next step, you will need to do some advance planning and preparation with a friend. You will first need to examine a survey map of your own house and property or that of a friend to find exactly where the water and waste pipes cross the lawn or sidewalk and enter the house. The problem will be to find the precise location and depth beneath the surface for each of those pipes, the pipe diameter, and even the material of which each is composed. If this information is not on the survey map of the property in question and you or your friend do not know exactly where those pipes are located or anything about them, don't despair. There are ways to search for clues: (1) check the basement or crawl-space to see where the pipes enter the house; (2) look for shut-off valves near the main water line; and (3) check village or town or city maps for the water and sewer systems and find the locations of pipe connections and junctions. These junctions are often indicated by triangulation from significant points and are accurately defined. Either these records or those of the local utility companies can then tell you the size of the pipes and their depth. Using this information, you will then be able to draw your own map of the area to be dowsed and record on it the location, depth, material, and size of each of your targets.

PRACTICE: KNOWN SITE

Once you have all of the pertinent information and have become generally familiar with it, go to the location and begin your dowsing search.

Remember that one of the first steps you practiced in learning to dowse was to create an image of the target so clear that you could then dowse it as if it actually existed. In this next step you will be seeking a target that actually exists. Furthermore, it is a target of which you know the location and the characteristics. At the same time that you visualize *exactly* what it is you are seeking, as you did during that first step, you will now be concentrating on the idea of the target *in place*. You will create a mental image of the water pipe that corresponds as nearly as possible to the actual pipe.

First stand to one side of that general area of the property and hold your L-rods or Y-rod in the search position, as in Figure 11. Create the image of a water pipe and ask, "In what direction do I need to walk to find the water pipe beneath this lawn?" Then, holding your dowsing device in the search position, slowly turn your body in clockwise and counterclockwise arcs as you scan the area to be dowsed. If you are using your Y-rod, you will feel

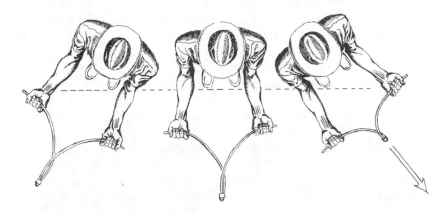

Figure 11. Holding the Y-rod in the search position, the dowser turns his body until the rod snaps down when he is facing the target he has programmed himself to find.

the tug as you begin to face the correct direction. It will snap downward when you are exactly facing the direction of the target. If you use your L-rods, you will find that they will remain "locked on" to the target you have in mind, continuing to point toward the target no matter how you turn your body (Figure 12). This indication will at first be only a general one, especially since your target covers a large area, but as you continue to swivel back and forth, the location of your target will be indicated with increasing precision. You may find it easier to use only one L-rod instead of both, holding it at the end of your outstretched arm, treating it as an extension of your arm.

It *does not matter* that you already know the direction; you are training yourself so that at the desired time, when the image and the target coincide, your dowsing device will give the response that you've already programmed. You should use all the information that you know about the target to practice (1) asking the right question and (2) visualizing the precise image. When you later practice on an unknown target, your mind, through the medium of the right question or specific image, will gradually develop the ability to establish a resonance with the target, and your dowsing rod, as a readout device for your mind, will give the appropriate response.

After you do successfully receive a response to your first question and know the direction of the target, return your dowsing tool to the search mode, or position, and walk toward the target. At the same time, hold the image of a water pipe firmly in mind. When you reach the target, in this case the water pipe, you will receive the same responses that you did when your dowsing tool passed over the edge of your desk or chair— provided, of course, that you are able to hold the idea of the specific target clearly in mind. If you are using L-rods, they should return to the search position as you pass beyond the pipe; if you are concentrating solely, specifically, and accurately on the idea of your target, you should be able to pass over any other kind of pipe or any underground veins of water with no response from the rods.

It is all a matter of selectivity, which may take some time to develop, but it is also a question of how exact and specific you can make your question or image. For example, your property

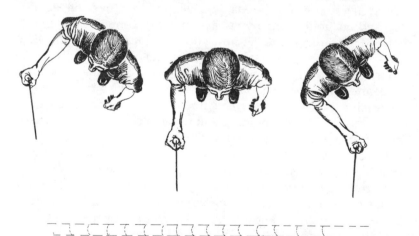

Figure 12. No matter which way the dowser turns, the L-rod continues to point toward the target.

may have two water pipes, one presently in use and one obsolete. You may ask for the location of the water pipe and have a clear mental image of it, but you may locate the obsolete one, or even both of them. You therefore should refine your question to ask for the water pipe that is in service *now*. If you do so, then with a little practice you will be able to pass over the obsolete pipe with no response from your dowsing rods.

SPECIFIC QUESTIONS

Once you locate the pipe, verify its location with the information you already have. Then stand over it and ask a series of specific questions. You will find it easiest to begin with the dowsing tool that gives the liveliest response to your questions. (You will want to practice with all three tools eventually.) First place your dowsing tool in the search mode and ask, "How deep below the surface of the lawn is the center (or top) of the water pipe?" Count down in feet and inches from the surface until, with practice, your dowsing tool responds at the correct depth. Once again, use the information you already have researched to verify your dowsing. If you are not on target, then go through the process again, this time gently urging yourself to produce the appropriate response at the correct depth.

Next you ask, mentally or aloud, "What is the water pipe made of?" Name different materials — copper, iron, plastic — until you receive a response. If you take the time to visualize each of the materials in turn clearly, the response will eventually occur when your visualization matches the actual material. You may also ask, "What is the diameter of the pipe?" and count fractions of an inch until you get a response. Likewise, if you create an image of a pipe of the appropriate size as you count those fractions, the response should occur when the image you have created matches the actual size of the pipe.

After you have received verifiable responses on the property site with the water pipe, practice the same procedure with the waste pipe. Start again at the side of the property and scan as you did before, again moving your body in an arc, this time asking for the direction you should walk to find the waste pipe. Remember to make sure that you are holding a clear image of it being presently in use. Continue to scan until your dowsing tool locks on to the appropriate direction, and then walk toward the target as you did while searching for the water pipe. Since this pipe is larger, it will make a greater difference whether you program your dowsing rod to respond to the leading edge or the center of the pipe. Also, be sure that you know whether the response indicates that you have reached the target with the point of your rod, with your hands, or with your feet. Once that is clear, then proceed with the other questions—depth, material, size—in the same manner that you did with the water pipe.

You should practice obtaining these responses until you are able to match them exactly with the information that you have already obtained about your site. Remember that if you do not get a precise response, you should gently urge your dowsing device to move correctly when you reach the known site or ask the appropriate question. You may have to move the device consciously until that motion becomes automatic. When you do so, be sure that you stand directly over the pipe and hold its image clearly in your mind.

As we have stressed, everyone is a "natural" dowser, but some people have to remove innate disbelief before they can claim and develop this natural ability. If your response is not precise, remember that you are still a beginner and are still entraining yourself to a way of thinking and responding that may be entirely new, and you therefore have to remind yourself not only of the nature of the signals themselves, but also of the appropriate responses.

PRACTICE: UNKNOWN SITE

You should practice at a site already known to you until you can receive consistently correct answers to your questions with no conscious effort on your part. The next step is to go through the same series of questions and searches at another verifiable location—an altogether different property would be a good choice. Go through the same search procedures and series of questions at this new site. This time, however, locate the pipes and indicate your responses to the questions on a map that you draw as you are dowsing. When finished, you can check your dowsed findings against known information. How accurate were your findings?

If your answers differ from that information, use the errors as learning opportunities. Consider several things that could have interfered to cause these errors:

(1) You received an authentic response, but not to the target you were seeking. This error can be corrected by concentrating more fully on the *specific* target and avoiding a response to any other pipes or water veins. For example, if you were searching for a water pipe and received a response where no pipe was indicated, you may have located an underground vein of flowing water. This would indicate that you had successfully held the idea of water, but you hadn't refined it to the idea of water in a pipe.

(2) You allowed your rational mind to step in to determine, incorrectly, where it thought the pipe really ought to be. This does not have to be a conscious interference. You may be responding to visual clues on the property that are entirely off base, or you may have a set of preconceptions that destroy any opportunity for effective resonance between your mental image and the actual target. Pipes to houses, particularly older houses, can be found laid at all sorts of unexpected angles. You are always better off making no assumptions at all.

(3) Your mind may have wandered from the question or the image. This situation is the most difficult one of all to correct, because most of us are not used to concentrating or focusing on one thing for any length of time. This can be corrected by regular additional practice in holding the appropriate idea or image or question in your mind. If the image changes, your target may also change and give you an incorrect response.

If you have made errors at the second site, you should determine their nature to the best of your ability. Then go back and dowse the second site again, this time treating it as you did the first site; that is, determine the actual locations and characteristics of the targets by reference to the site map. If you do that, you can then hold not only the image in mind for each target, but also the precise physical information. This continual practice on targets for which you have immediate verification is important.

We do want to stress again that above all else you must avoid feeling discouraged if you get wrong answers when you dowse. Dowsing is really like many other activities, because you can learn from mistakes, and each one of those mistakes must be understood as being a positive step forward in the refinement of your dowsing skill. It is also important that you make the effort to try to understand *why* any particular mistake occurred. What were you thinking at the time? Had your mind strayed from its image of the target? Had you made any incorrect assumptions? Realize that even though you may have made a mistake, you did receive a response to something. Your goal is to determine what that "something" was and why it was an error. The problem you are facing is not one of whether you can dowse or not; it is one of the refinement and clarity of the question you formulate and the image you hold as you go through the physical dowsing process. The answer is always latent in the question.

The steps so far—working with known, verifiable targets— ensure that you will develop the necessary basic skills and unique patterns of thinking. These patterns will ultimately give you not only confidence in your dowsing ability, but also the capacity to see mistakes as opportunities. If you take advantage of these opportunities, you will gain a deeper understanding of the process involved in mastering the skill of dowsing.

In order to help you understand the dowsing process, we will suggest a paradigm for dowsing that will serve to clarify and ground the basic processes that you have begun to develop. First, however, we will put dowsing into a historical perspective.

PART II

GROUNDING THE DIVINING PROCESS

What we call empty space contains an immense background of energy; matter as we know it is a small, "quantized" wavelike excitation on top of this background, rather like a tiny ripple on a vast sea.

—David Bohm

Day and night, the Sea keeps on churning the foam. You behold the foam but not the sea—how strange!

—Jalaluddin Rumi
(13th century)

6

Historical Perspective

Dowsing is an activity that has played a part in the everyday life of people for a very long time. In this chapter we want to look briefly at some of those activities, and we want to see (1) the manner by which various changes of perspective in the field of dowsing correlate with the changing perspectives within historical epochs and (2) how they relate to the evolvement of our personal range of consciousness. As we develop our dowsing skill and create a paradigm to increase our present understanding of dowsing, we also begin to rediscover something that is part of our own roots, part of our own encoded pattern of being—a part of our human heritage that lies beyond the reach of our conscious memories. We do not intend to give a formal history of dowsing in this chapter, but we will examine some of the shifting attitudes toward it and suggest a perspective from which we may examine these attitudes.

We start with a few of the earliest indications of dowsing. With a date of 6000 B.C. attributed to it, a rock painting in the Sahara Desert near Tassili in southern Algeria shows a man walking behind cattle. He has a forked stick in his hand and is holding it in a way that most dowsers do today, with the rod angled upward, and he is surrounded by interested spectators. It is different from the usual pictures of herdsman, because something else of interest seems to be going on. The one factor that is different is the forked stick.

This painting by itself would mean little, except that it is one example of other ancient drawings and sculptures that can be found scattered throughout the world. According to Francis Hitching (see Appendix E for references to books by Hitching and Christopher Bird), there are in Peru, for example, said to be rock carvings over 2000 years old that likewise depict what appears to be the practice of dowsing. Egyptian sculptures from the same period show a priest holding a forked twig, and the Great Pyramid of Gizeh, said by archaeologists to have been built between the second and third millennia B.C. (although psychics date it as far older than that), contains many dowsable features, critical to its location, that have been found by members of the American Society of Dowsers. Abraham's Well, dug during the Bronze Age, is over 100 feet deep in solid rock, with a clear, cold stream running directly at its bottom. These are only a few suggestive examples, and beyond these we can look for further evidence from the Hittites, the Greeks, the early Romans, and the Chinese (see Appendix F, the annotated Selected Bibliography, for indications of where to look further).

The evidence from those ancient times indicates that various forms of dowsing were apparently a part of man's activities, perhaps more naturally realized at those times because of the greater sense of wholeness, or connectedness, felt by early man toward his environment and his identity with it. He may indeed have considered himself and his environment as one unit, mutually bound by subtle threads of awareness that shaped every aspect of his life. When this affinity was most highly developed, external dowsing devices may have been unnecessary. If these suggestions are correct, then as man passed through further periods of development, his attunement to the more subtle aspects of his environment may have lessened, so that he needed a separate device to identify characteristics of the world about him that were at one time instinctively grasped and understood.

During modern eras this awareness seemed to have been disregarded and lost, a change that coincided with the rise of materialism. Dowsing and dowsing-related activities then became a special interest, practiced under sponsorship, or guardedly, or in the most elementary and uninformed and isolated way. An assumption can be made that a closely guarded position might well have been fostered, possibly with the noblest of intent, as a means of limiting knowledge to those who might not destroy it. (Such, after all, was the basis of the *guru–chela* system of India and Tibet that passed knowledge from the master to student in a special relationship.) The rod and the scepter became mere symbols—metaphors often enough for the misuse of the power and wisdom they originally represented.

The practice of dowsing, at its best naturally creative, became a repetitious activity lost in history's byways. Because it had become the knowledge of the few, it lacked support for the dynamic and creative role that we envision for it in this book.

We can find evidence of this decline in comments made by some of the early religious leaders. In the seventh century St. Theodore of Canterbury condemned "augury and divination." In the sixteenth century Martin Luther included the use of the rod in his list of acts in violation of the First Commandment. Even today there are some sects whose leaders consider dowsing the "work of the devil" (one of the popular terms for dowsing is "water witching"), just as there are, likewise, those who use the art of dowsing to satisfy the little "I," that egocentric self that is attracted to power. The mind set is still with us. It will be met and must be reckoned with in the apprenticeship of any dowser.

The origin of this condemnation is, at least in part, bound up with the duality between two essential issues: (1) personal and independent freedom and (2) dependence on the power and authority of the specialist, government or otherwise. If one opts for opinion based on the assumed authority of another, one is opting for limitation, which means that one may also be opting for severance from one's own source. If this is his mind view, the dowser becomes less able to use his dowsing to enlarge his own consciousness and develop a harmonious path of service and wholeness beyond that little "I." Conversely, if his dowsing stems entirely from personal and selfish motivation, he defeats the thrust and loses the benefits of his art.

Although dowsing has been condemned, isolated, and misunderstood, it did not vanish as an art. For one reason, it was a natural human talent; for another, it was too practical. In sixteenth century Germany, Martin Luther notwithstanding, dowsing was commonly used for the mining of ore, simply because it was such an efficient tool. To be on the safe side, however, those German dowsers did everything they could to make it acceptable. Each dowser wore a distinctive uniform as a member of the mining hierarchy. There are records of incantations recited by those early dowsers so that all could be assured that dowsing was in agreement and harmony with the mores of the time. Even the Church itself from time to time authorized members of its own priesthood to dowse and divine.

Because of its usefulness, and despite the official caution from the Church, dowsing continued to be something that was welcomed and accepted. In the 1500s, when Queen Elizabeth I sought new sources of tin, zinc, copper, and gold in Cornwall, she imported German dowsers. According to Dr. Zaboj Harvalik, writing in *The American Dowser* in 1973, the very words "dowser" and "dowse" may be a corruption of the Old High German *deutzen*, which means "to locate, to find."

The coming of the Age of Reason and the Industrial Revolution was accompanied by the writings of the natural philosophers whose understanding of man and the universe often reflected mechanistic and materialistic principles. This era was a great time for peering through microscopes and telescopes, recording, analyzing, and developing fixed laws of nature from observations and deductions made by the use of a process considered to be man's hope—systematized Scientific Method. The knowledge of the physical world gained by this method persuaded these thinkers to view man as a limited being whose actions were determined by behavioristic principles. His intuitive side was treated with more and more skepticism. Dowsing, as an expression of intuition, did not fit the prevailing rationalistic concepts, just as it did not lend itself to systematized methods of verification. Many concluded, therefore, that dowsing was quackery and believed dowsers were at best deluded, or at worst downright charlatans. This view of dowsing and dowsers is one that has persisted to our own time, and it is lodged in the minds of many conventional thinkers who see themselves as rational and clear-headed people. They create in their minds a logical world in which dowsing cannot exist, and so for them it does not exist, whatever evidence may exist to the contrary.

The concepts and theories being developed at the leading edge of science in the "new physics" and the "new biology" are beginning to reinforce the concept of man existing in a holistic, cocreative relationship with the planet. There is a new climate and understanding within which dowsing may unfold as a potential that lies dormant in all of us, which can be accessed in natural, progressive stages by all who are willing to go through a systematic self-training.

This expanding awareness, we feel, is a sign of a return to a relationship with the cosmos that was once a normal part of ancient existence. We are now able to add to this classic consciousness the material knowledge that has been gained and has become part of our modern heritage, including the most recent insights into the nature of reality. We can open the doors of dowsing to wider vistas than could have been comprehended before. If we accept the new paradigm that the essential codes of all creation lie within each of us, we sense that no matter how many doors to this new-old knowledge we open, an infinite number of other doors appear to us. That is why dowsing is such an exciting skill to learn and develop. In no other age in history would we have been able to expand it as we can now.

In order that you may gain the concepts to allow an appropriate expansion of awareness to take place within your own minds, we next suggest a model that may provide a basis for understanding the nature of the phenomenon we have called dowsing.

7

Toward A
Dowsing Paradigm

Once you become known as a dowser, one of the first questions you will be asked is, "What makes it work?" The question is fair enough, because dowsing is a process that does work; furthermore our culture is accustomed to explanations when things work and demands to understand a process and know its causes. The difficulty in the case of dowsing is that there are no ready-made or readily understood ways to answer that question. If you were to ask five old-time dowsers for explanations, you would probably receive five different answers, none of which would help you very much. A sixth might comment, "It doesn't matter to me how or why it works; it does, and that's good enough for me." That sixth dowser does avoid making any statements that may limit the concept of what he does, but for our purpose that kind of pragmatic response is not enough. Whether he admits it or not, he does have some concept of how dowsing works, though he prefers not to put it into words. He, like the other five dowsers, is working within a paradigm, and the odds are very high that it is a paradigm that will in some way limit his use of dowsing.

We feel it *does* matter how you think about dowsing, that an understanding of the how and why is important if you wish to develop your dowsing skill to its greatest potential. Once you begin your dowsing journey, the horizon you are able to establish for yourself will be limited only by the notion you have of it. If you are not aware of the implications of your definition, you may find you have unwittingly created your own barriers to future advancement or, even more damaging, have begun to drift into a world of fantasy. The concept that you accept must be clear and based on something meaningful and solid.

Let's consider some of the ways that people may think about dowsing. A well driller may say, "Naturally you get an accurate dowsing response; all you do is pick up visual clues from the land." If that driller then practiced dowsing, he might become pretty good at getting a reaction, but that reaction would be essentially in response to those visual clues. For him, visual clues might then become his limitation, and the limitation would continue as long as his concept of dowsing continued to be based solely on things visual. A classical scientist might say, "You know, when you learn to dowse, all you do is train yourself to respond to electromagnetic signals or gravitational fluctuations." His concept might be a bit more sophisticated, but if that scientist were then to learn to dowse, his response to electromagnetic signals or the magnetic gradient would define the limits he has imposed on his dowsing. At the furthest extreme someone whose concept is unfocused might say, "Dowsing carries me into the infinite and allows me to to dip into another dimension and emerge with the secrets of the Cosmic Source." Granted, that could be construed as an airy way of wording an advanced level of dowsing, but it is woefully inadequate because it is unbalanced. Because of its vagueness there is the possibility that the dowser might begin dowsing little more than his or her own fantasies. That dowser would then be giving unwitting and misleading verification to his own personal delusions.

In order to avoid limitations and lack of grounding, we base our approach on the following three standards:

1. It is important to develop a clear concept of dowsing.
2. We must accept the fact that no matter what concept we develop, it will be a temporary and limited one.
3. We are willing to revise and enlarge that concept when it becomes appropriate to do so.

The first step we feel it is appropriate to take in developing an adequate concept of dowsing is to move into the domain of physics and consider the nature, not of matter, but of empty space. That's the term most of us use when we talk about the so-called nonmaterial segment of the universe, which includes everything from the space between the stars to the space between the parts of an atom. Our conventional concept of empty space results from the manner of thinking to which we have been conditioned. It is a "true" manner of thinking, but only so from one specific point of view. When we look at it from a different point of view, we discover that what we call empty space is not all that empty. According to post-Newtonian physics—quantum and postquantum physics—all of that so-called empty space really contains, or rather really *is*, an immense background of wavelike patterns of enfolded energy.

We can understand that concept more clearly by means of two simple comparisons. Consider, for example, the antenna on our radio or television receiver. It makes contact with a very small area of physical space, yet if we turn the set on and move the dial, we have access to the full range of radio or television signals, limited only by the sensitivity of the antenna and the sophistication of our receiver. All those signals that are created throughout the world exist within that tiny segment of space, and yet each is unique and can be picked up in all its complexity by that simple antenna and identified individually by an adjustment of the receiver.

Next let's consider a common experiment that you may have performed in a physics class. You take a thin, rather large, flat metal disc and anchor it so that any single note of music directed at it causes it to vibrate. Then you cover it with a thin layer of fine sand. When you sound the note, the sand will form into specific patterns which change as you change the note. For our purposes the important point is that when the vibration begins, the sand moves to the areas on the disc that produce the *least* vibration. The greater the energy of vibration, the more quickly certain areas will become clear of sand and the more precisely the patterns will be defined.

We can extend the implications of that experiment, in which we created patterns on a metal disc, to a much more complex, multidimensional level. At this more complex level we may consider those patterns on the metal disc as analogous to the one aspect of energy, or vibration, which we call matter. In

Wholeness and the Implicate Order (London, Routledge & Kegan Paul, 1980), physicist David Bohm suggests that even though objects formed out of these patterns of matter may seem very solid to us, this matter consists of small, quantized wavelike patterns of excitation forming on top of, or emerging out of, a background of energy, like tiny ripples forming on the surface of the sea. Although we are commonly aware only of the matter around us or the matter that forms us, modern theories indicate that it may very well be the background that is the basic, or the primary, level of energy, somewhat in the manner that it was in those empty spaces between the patterns on the metal disc.

To understand this model, we can think of ourselves, not as dense, solid beings, but as complex material formations evolving out of the pure energy of those quantized, wavelike patterns. In themselves these individual bits of matter that are created and that seem so solid do not really amount to all that much, either. In *The Eye of Shiva* (New York, William Morrow & Co., 1981), Amaury de Riencourt suggested that if all the nuclei of all the atoms that make up the whole of mankind were packed tightly together, their global aggregate would be about the size of a large grain of rice.

If we view those atoms through the perspective of experimental physics, we begin to see ourselves not as dense, solid beings, but instead as composed mostly of nothing at all, or at least nothing that is material and observable. We and the objects around us are not solids but lacy patterns extending through as yet undefined areas of incalculable energy. According to Dr. Bohm, these lacy patterns of energy are formations of what he calls an explicate order of reality, or a secondary reality, somewhat analogous to the music that comes from our radios or the sand patterns that formed from the energy transmitted by musical notes. That is, the here-and-now reality has been transformed from wavelike energies that abound in another state. Rather than being the essential reality, then, this explicate order is more like a local effect creating a limited sense of order. Behind this order, or this local effect, lies that other exceedingly subtle but all-pervasive order of enfolded energy that Bohm calls the implicate order, or primary reality. This enfolded order of reality is furthermore involved in a two-way process, in that it not only creates the secondary reality, which is our conventional concept of reality, but it continually reabsorbs the essence of all the subatomic particles that exist in that reality simultaneously with the process of continually creating new particles.

According to this theory the enfolding and unfolding go on constantly and dynamically and creatively beyond time, because this primary reality exists ultimately not only everywhere but everywhen, as an eternal matrix that is not only spaceless but timeless, containing at once all of those aspects and patterns of reality that we would perceive as the past, present, and future.

This may sound complex, but it is akin to the state of our own minds, which also carry as an eternal "now" all our past memories, present experiences, and tendencies for the future. Within the "now" of our minds, we are able to shape those past memories, present experiences, and possible future developments into a creative pattern.

We now want to take one more step and consider an idea popularized by the late Itzhak Bentov, author of *Stalking the Wild Pendulum* (Rochester, VT, Destiny Books, 1987). He suggests that we think of this vast sea that lies behind our concept of the created universe not as a sea of energy, but rather as a sea of consciousness—a sea of awareness, or thought, or intention. In his view it is this consciousness that, when put into a vibratory state, manifests as matter, from which the different forms we see around us are made. According to this approach, everything around you—your table or desk, your plants, even your own body—is made up of rapidly vibrating consciousness.

IMPORTANCE TO DOWSERS

From these large concepts of the nature of creation, we are now in a position to develop a new concept of ourselves, one that eventually becomes of critical importance to our successful development as dowsers. First, we may now think of ourselves as conscious beings awash in a sea of energy that not only is a part of us, but that *is* us; and second, at the same time this sea of energy is itself also a sea of consciousness, which on one level defines a specific part of us while at the same time, on another level, it is the whole of us, our essential selves, intimately associated with the greater universe around us.

We need to remember, as the theorists themselves remind us, that the nature of this enfolded sea of consciousness is beyond any limited comprehension that we are able to give it. Yet out of it is created all matter, all forms, and all beings. It is furthermore a concept that recognizes the innate power of this enfolded energy, since every iota of it contains the totality. A cubic centimeter of our so-called empty space, say these modern theorists, contains more enfolded energy than all created matter in the entire material universe.

We are not aware of this power in our ordinary state, of course, because our level of awareness has the limitations of our material state. All the information that comes into our bodies and emerges into our consciousness does so (at least in our ordinary state of consciousness) through the severely limiting and objectifying medium of our senses. Sometimes we misunderstand the nature of this selective information that comes to us. When we look at something, for example, we may forget that we do not see the object itself, and that we are actually seeing a pattern of reflected wave forms within a certain frequency range. This frequency range, which is the only one to which we have been accustomed to respond, is limited, and it becomes even more limited during the process of seeing. These vibratory patterns pass through the lenses of our eyes and excite the optic receptors. We then select certain aspects from these abstract excitations and give them shape and meaning by accepting and placing them in relation to limited aspects of other abstractions already encoded in our brain. Our subsequent potential for reaching into these fragmentary abstract patterns and giving them a meaningful shape is really quite good, however, because the brain tends to store the incoming frequencies in a holographic manner, so that bits of awareness are scattered throughout the brain in a continual pattern of interaction. Experiments have shown that those pulses of information from all our senses, not just our eyes, are stored, or enfolded, throughout our minds as frequency patterns, and the brain acts in part like a frequency analyzer as it sorts through the patterns and unfolds the information back into the secondary system of forms and memories and thoughts that we can recognize or that we can create from this enfolded knowledge.

The scientific model that we have outlined briefly above may offer us clues for creating a model for an understanding of dowsing. Once we do understand this scientific model, we will also understand how dowsing allows us to move beyond the limitations of our brains and create a condition by which we may access the sea of enfolded knowledge, or consciousness, that surrounds and permeates us all the time, whether we choose to be aware of it or not.

We can discover more clues that relate to the working of this model in studies of brain-wave patterns. These are customarily separated into four different frequency ranges—beta, alpha, theta, and delta. Beta is the range generally between 14 and 30 hertz, or cycles per second, and is most active during normal waking activity. It is therefore the one most generally associated with the conventional states of everyday consciousness.

Below the beta range is alpha, generally defined as 8–13 hertz, a band of frequencies generally associated with tranquil or passive states of mind. It can exist both when we are experiencing feelings of peace and contentment, and when we are relaxed in gentle meditation. Next is theta, 4–7 hertz, the frequencies found during those sleep states that produce dreams. Theta corresponds to the state in which creative ideas and "instant" solutions to problems can flourish, and from which our material concerns are largely banished. The lowest frequency range is delta, $1/4$–4 hertz. It is the range of very deep sleep in which dreams and images are absent. It is also active during the more profound states of meditation and superconscious perception.

Keep in mind that these brain-wave frequencies are only *indications* of activity, not the activity itself, and do not explain anything about the nature of that activity, although they do relate to various specific states of consciousness that have been observed in the scientific laboratory. In examining how brain waves may relate to the art of dowsing, we must acknowledge the seminal work of an English doctor, Maxwell Cade, who for

45 years brought his training and expertise as physicist, engineer, martial-arts student, and meditator to bear on defining
states of consciousness (see Maxwell Cade and Nona Coxhead,
The Awakened Mind, Element Books Ltd, United Kingdom, 1987).
With the aid of Geoffrey Blundell in 1976, a double electro-
encephalograph (or EEG) was developed to measure the frequencies that occurred in each half of the brain. Working with
this sensitive instrument, and in the course of training more
than 3000 students, Cade determined the relation of deep sleep
to delta, dreaming sleep to theta, reverie to alpha-theta, awareness to beta-alpha-theta-delta, and the various combinations of
different frequency ranges of brain waves and physical body
states to a variety of altered states of consciousness. This unique
and pioneering work was continued in 1983 by Edith Jurka, a
medical doctor specializing in psychiatry, as part of her research
on mind development techniques. As a result, important light
has been shed on the phenomenon of dowsing.

Tests carried out by Dr. Jurka (see *The American Dowser*, 23:1,
1983) indicated that during the actual process of dowsing there
is an increase in the microvoltage the brain produces in the
alpha frequencies, an increase measurable even in the novice
dowser. It is noteworthy that the dowser makes no conscious
effort to enter a meditative state. The information recorded by
the EEG suggests that the brain responds naturally in the dowsing process just as it would to a meditative practice designed to
increase personal awareness. Furthermore, as the dowser gains
experience or as he or she engages in more subtle levels of
dowsing, the frequencies intensify in theta. Recall that theta is
the range in which ideas begin to unfold into images, the range
that involves prototypal forms. Finally, as we will see, the functioning dowser may reflect the delta state as well. Dr. Jurka also
discovered that experienced dowsers seem to remain in alpha
and theta whether they are actually dowsing or not.

More remarkable yet, talented dowsers who have been tested
exhibited activity in all four ranges—beta, alpha, theta, and delta
(the so-called state 5 condition)—*all at the same time*, something
that apparently not even the accomplished yogi can exhibit
when he performs his *siddhis* or paranormal wonders. These

dowsers are combining the beta frequency, which is used alone during ordinary consciousness, with brain frequencies that usually are active only in the absence of ordinary consciousness. This suggests that the dowser is using a larger portion of his potential on all of those measurable levels of activity in a perfectly balanced and natural way. It is the condition, apparently, that characterizes his far-seeing, far-knowing, and far-doing, as well as ultimately his cooperation with nature.

A difficulty faced by the beginning dowser—and also by many of the more experienced dowsers—is that the individual ordinarily has no concept of dowsing as a progressive art, and may have no idea how to relate these states of increased activity within his bio-system to the scope of his powers. We feel that it is important, especially for beginners, to approach dowsing with responsibility and to attempt to master each level of competence, as we suggest in this book. The succeeding subtleties will then be much more readily grasped and incorporated within his practice.

Let's consider one example that underscores the need for good grounding and careful preparation in dowsing. Because of the nature of our planet, we all live in a resonating cavity. It is the cavity that exists between the ionosphere and the surface of the earth, and it resonates with a fundamental frequency of about 7.8 hertz. This is the frequency that lies at the lower end of the alpha range closest to theta, and furthest from the beta of alert consciousness. It is the alpha frequency which is enhanced during our ordinary dowsing activity. It would therefore seem that as we develop our dowsing skill and increase our mental capacity in alpha and theta, we become increasingly in tune, or in resonance, with a basic frequency of our planet, *and it happens whether we want it to or not and whether we are prepared to be in tune or not.* The risk for the unprepared, or ungrounded, dowser is that these subtle but verifiable changes can produce not only a state of unmastered sensitivity but also something even more dangerous, an illusion of personal power. If this sensitivity remains unmastered because of careless preparation, the dowser may open himself to various difficulties. For example, he may become acutely uncomfortable around everyday electrical systems, because those electrical systems, which constantly radiate their pulsing energy, operate at various harmonics of this fundamental frequency; or he may experience discomfort during atmospheric disturbances, during which the characteristics of the resonating cavity are altered. In addition, attention paid to that little "I" of the personal ego may result in an unwarranted sense of special accomplishment or even spiritual pride. These traps are insidious, and they can destroy the mental state that would allow the dowser to advance smoothly through all the stages of dowsing. In other words, because of the increased sensitivity the dowser gains, as indicated by EEG experiments, the undisciplined or ungrounded learner may unwittingly create the very conditions that block his further development. Advanced stages of dowsing are appropriate for us only if we approach them with patience and common sense. In this connection, we think it significant that Maxwell Cade found that those whom he measured who exhibited a strong bilaterally symmetrical beta-alpha-theta combination during their everyday activities were responsive to the needs of others, and had a genuine love of humanity and a desire to serve. He felt it was the result of a spiritual (though not necessarily religious) life style. Dr. Jurka feels that the special thing about the talented dowsers is that while dowsing, they have that wide delta plus the full beta of consciousness. It is also very important that the right and left brains put out similar voltages—that they are coordinated.

The advantage of following a program of disciplined preparation and practice becomes even more clear when we examine one more change in us that may take place as we dowse. Dr. Jurka's investigations suggest that over a period of time, as we master increasingly subtle problems of dowsing, our EEG readings show higher voltage in the frequencies theta and delta. Theta is the range in which vivid, lifelike images ordinarily appear only in the unconscious sleeping mind and a frequency range that, in the conscious state, has heretofore been available only to those who have mastered Eastern meditation techniques after years of continued discipline. We stress the point again that this is one of those states that may be achieved by the dowser *irrespective of his or her desire or preparation*.

IMPORTANCE OF DELTA

This state, indicated by increased microvoltages in delta, has sometimes been popularized as the one of so-called cosmic consciousness, because the person achieving it through Eastern disciplines is able to release his ordinary sense of "self" and receive information of a nature that his five senses were not constructed to receive—just as in our conventional state of self-consciousness, we do not receive sound through our eyes or taste through our ears. This concept takes on tremendous importance in terms of the model we are developing. We suggest that this increase in delta indicates that the dowser is at the level at which the small sea of knowledge enfolded in holograph-like wave patterns within his mind is able to achieve resonance with the vast sea of conscious energy enfolded in a similar mode throughout the universe in a timeless and spaceless eternal now.

This does not mean that when we dowse we have all this information come to us at once in one great, smashing breakthrough. It does mean that if we master the art of dowsing systematically through appropriate steps, we may ultimately become able to achieve this resonance with the enfolded order of primary reality *at will*.

We have stressed the importance of asking the right question and holding the idea of that question clearly in mind when we dowse. If you, as a conscientious dowser, do accept the model that we are developing, then you must realize that as you dowse, not only are you already in contact with this vast sea of enfolded reality, but this vast sea is the essential part of your makeup and always has been. To put it another way, *we "know" the answers to our questions before we ask them even if we do not have immediate access to this "knowing."* To have access to such a piece of knowledge, we must go through the ritual of tuning our minds to the right combination of frequencies (which to an experienced dowser happens immediately when he creates the intent to dowse). This ritualization is an objectification of a subjective experience that (1) bypasses the rational mind, (2) is transformed into a wavelike pattern of energy, (3) achieves resonance with a specific phase of the enfolded order, and (4) unfolds the pattern that becomes the answer from a suitable but authentic source.

With this model we can begin to understand that, on one hand, each of us is a fraction of the universe, linked with all the other fractions of the universe by resonance. At the same time, however, we are also the totality of the universe. For the dowser all knowledge becomes fair game under conditions that are truly resonant. The code for understanding these conditions lies within, and dowsing allows us access to this code.

8

The American Society
of Dowsers

The French practitioners call it radiesthesia, and eastern Europeans use the terms bioenergetics and the bio-physical effect. Both groups have their associations and societies. In England and the United States it is called dowsing, and the most prominent organization involved with it in the United States is The American Society of Dowsers, which marked its silver anniversary at a convention in 1985.

Founded as an informal group of hobbyists, ASD has slowly been growing in the direction of a professionally minded organization. Since its beginning it has been responsible for setting standards for its nationwide network of chapters and members. In keeping with its democratic beginnings, however, it is still made up primarily of volunteer amateurs. Even with this makeup, from its earliest days it has conscientiously worked to promote both the advancement of the knowledge of dowsing as a whole and the capacity of its individual members to progress in a disciplined, responsible manner. Its conventions and chapter meetings, however, still usually carry more of the character of small-town get-togethers than professional convocations. Also, like many such organizations that have grown from small beginnings, it has had its growing pains. It does, however, survive these setbacks and, at least at this present writing, continues to grow in respectability and credibility.

The Society began in a modest way, as one of the events in a New England small town fall foliage festival. Hank Balivet, a local mover and shaker in Danville, Vermont, promoted the festival in 1958. To provide a unique added attraction he decided to round up some country dowsers for the visitors to see. After all, dowsing was a skill dating back to the colonial days of Danville, and no early colonist in his right mind, in Danville or elsewhere, would have dug a well without first consulting the local dowser.

There were local dowsers at the festival, like Reg Smith and Clint Gray of Danville, but there was also an executive from General Electric at Schenectady, New York, a lawyer from Manhattan, a corporate V.P. from New Jersey—in short, a cross section of every level of society drawn together by Balivet's invitation, overjoyed to find each other, and eager to tell each other of different ways the dowsing response could be put to good use.

After they had met informally for three more years during those fall foliage festivals, one member of that early group, Galen Hutchison, a distinguished lawyer who had moved to Vermont from New Jersey, drew up a set of by-laws and submitted it to his fellow dowsers for approval. In 1961 the American Society of Dowsers came into being as a Vermont corporation with the simplest of corporate goals, the study and sharing of dowsing through the formation of a scientific and educational society. In later years lawyer Hutchison succeeded in winning a tax-exempt status for ASD, and from the original meeting of eighteen souls, the membership has now grown to nearly four thousand, with over sixty chapters scattered across the country. Some members would still like ASD to retain the cracker-barrel atmosphere it had when the total membership could sit comfortably in one room of the Danville town hall, but others, anxious to promote dowsing, are at work to expand its membership tenfold.

One factor aiding the credibility of ASD has been its record in print. The Society began to build this record in 1961 with the publication of a journal, *The American Dowser*. At first it was run off on a mimeograph machine on a Danville neighbor's back porch. Despite its church-bulletin appearance and its chatty style, those early issues contained surprisingly sophisticated thinking and good writing. Then in 1967 Ray Willey, a business executive from Schenectady, agreed to edit and supervise it, and by 1969 the journal acquired the professional format that it has today. At present four editors, all volunteers, take turns putting together the quarterly issues, which, taken together, contain a full spectrum of matters relating to the field of dowsing. Articles range from the speculative and theoretical to the scientific and anecdotal, but the material in each issue is now gathered from contributors around the world, for it is mailed to 42 countries and translated into Russian. Its increase in breadth has, however, also required a sacrifice of much of the informal chattiness of those early years, when everyone knew everyone else on a first-name basis.

Even with its two-hundred-fold growth, however, ASD is still made up primarily of those volunteer hobbyists. In its simplest form the Society provides pleasure and companionship for a number of people and brings them together in a common purpose. From its beginnings the Society has recognized that one of the keys to the expansion of dowsing to its fullest potential lies in the use of dowsing not as a vehicle for personal fame but for service. In addition, Galen Hutchison has said that the real purpose of dowsing—the inner purpose, if you will—is to provide a means for the raising of consciousness of all with whom it comes in contact. It is a purpose now becoming more strongly recognized within the Society and now understood as a natural outcome of that code of service.

The Society, formed as an "educational and scientific society" under the laws of Vermont, is not a trade organization. As a tax-exempt corporation, it does not engage in business for a profit and does not, under federal statute, lobby for anything. Individual members may, of course, say or do as they wish in their own names, as long as they do not give their own personal views as ones necessarily held by the Society. ASD recognizes and encourages the freedom of speech of all its members, but it also requires its members to carry an awareness of their own personal responsibility. The founding fathers of ASD, who wisely envisioned an expanding contact with the public, devised a Code of Ethics as a frame of reference so that all ASD members might, from time to time, reevaluate their own sense of personal responsibility. This Code of Ethics, presented below, helps with the sometimes knotty and increasingly complex relationships the Society and its members have with the media, the scientific community, and the general public.

Section 1. They shall be guided in all their relations by the highest standards of personal integrity.

Section 2. They shall uphold before the public at all times the dignity and the reputation of the Society.

Section 3. They shall avoid and discourage sensationalism, exaggeration, undignified and unwarranted statements, or misleading advertisements.

Section 4. They shall refuse to undertake, if compensation for such work is involved, work which may be of questionable value or result, without first advising as to the probability of success.

Section 5. They shall not use their membership in this Society as evidence of qualification as a dowser or as a measure of ability or proficiency.

Section 6. They shall not exhibit or use the name of this Society on any letterhead or stationery, nor on any personal or business cards, nor in any advertising of a personal, business, or professional nature.

Those six simple, sensible rules of observance are really six ways of looking at the same idea, and that idea has to do with honesty, reliability, and responsibility. Even though some members or groups of members may occasionally say or do things that endanger the credibility of ASD, the organization as a whole survives with its integrity more or less intact because of the wisdom of its founders and the dedication of a core of its members.

PART III

ADVANCED CONCEPTS IN DOWSING

*Most of us have grown up with the idea that our
minds and memories are located inside our brains.
But, perhaps our minds are not inside our brains:
rather, our brains may lie in the field of our minds.
Our perceptual world may be all around us—just
what it seems to be.*

—Rupert Sheldrake

*The visible world was made to correspond to the
world invisible and there is nothing in this world but
is a symbol of something in that other world.*

—al-Ghazzali
(11th century)

9

The Next Step

We have thus far progressed a little way along the path of dowsing, even though this little way has already extended far beyond the reach of almost all dowsers of only a generation ago. There is more to come, both in practice and explanation, but before we take the next step let's review where we have traveled.

THE STEPS SO FAR

We started with an introduction to the three most commonly used devices—the L-rod, the Y-rod, and the pendulum. Then, after we described the dowser's version of the origin and behavior of water, you practiced with each one of the devices on the *idea of water* and the image created by that idea. You then transferred the idea of water to the edge of your table or desk or to the back of your chair, and the devices responded to that target as if it were there in reality. Then we recommended and outlined ways for you to go on-site to locate a series of known targets. While dowsing on-site you received a response, not to the idea of, say, a water pipe, but to the idea of that same water pipe *in place*—a particular, specific, material water pipe in position, in the ground. We stressed that the response was not to the physical target itself, but rather to the image of the target you reconstructed in your own mind. You practiced until that image and your precise questions concerning it exactly matched the physical target. Then we developed a model that, we hope, will increasingly help you to understand the *nature* of dowsing and the responsibility that dowsing engenders.

Your enquiring mind will continue to develop the concept we

have stressed at every step of the dowsing process, that we are involving ourselves with the *idea* of our target. Perhaps, as we have already suggested, the entire binary computer-like game of "yes" and "no" is essentially a *mental* one. Perhaps we have begun to involve ourselves with an invisible, interdimensional game of hide-and-seek that extends far beyond our conventional concepts of reality. Is the answer we seek *always there*? Is the extent of our skill in dowsing just a question of awareness, of our discovering its nature and giving it shape and form? These are the appropriate questions, and we would answer "yes" to them. Didn't Einstein say that matter is congealed thought? Is the universe a thought? Is it what we earlier called consciousness? Perhaps we are simply resonating with little bits of it here and there as we delve into it with the far-reaching aptitude of our biosystems.

These observations inevitably bring us to a new view of ourselves and our environment, a view we share with a growing number of people, even though few of them are able to verify it first hand as you have been doing through your dowsing. You may call this new view a raising or enlarging of personal consciousness, or just a new way of looking at the everyday world, a nice awareness that inevitably brings a larger understanding and greater compassion in its train. If you choose, you may now begin to see what is actually there, behind the world of appearances, and it may follow that you will begin to make better decisions about everything—from the ripeness of a cantaloupe in the supermarket, to finding a pleasant place to live, or even ultimately about a *way* to live.

THE NEXT STEP

We move now to that next step, and it's a large one. In addition to the L-rod, the Y-rod, the pendulum, and other dowsing tools, there is another device that you might eventually discover, and that device is yourself—you and you alone.

Once you have been dowsing for any length of time as an on-site dowser, walking over the ground with your favorite device in the search position, something will begin to happen. You will realize that you *knew* the rod was going to dip before you got to the target. The realization might come one or two or three steps before the actual external and physical reaction. Something activated the neurons of your brain so that they relayed a message to you of instantaneous, *conscious knowing*. When this experience takes place, and you gain confidence in your knowing through its continued verification, you are then ready to move ahead to this next stage of the dowsing journey, remote dowsing up to the horizon, or even a third stage, remote dowsing over the horizon. You can then stand where you are and survey the field of interest even when it cannot be seen — scan it, so to speak, with your inner dowsing rod — without the kind of painstaking survey you were making before.

Later, when you are comfortable with over-the-horizon dowsing and have a record of accurate readings from this remote dowsing, another magic moment can await you. It may come to you because of a suddenly felt need. For example, someone you know well calls and says, "I'm afraid; Daddy's gone again; we can't find him. I thought perhaps with your dowsing. . . ." Such calls do come. Without thinking you pick up your dowsing tool, and the first question intuitively may be, "Is the man safe and well?"

Notice that you are not asking where the man is, which is the third stage of dowsing, for that sudden need has taken you in another direction, to a fourth stage; you are asking about his state, his vital forces at that particular instant. *You are making an intangible query.* If you have taken the time to develop a good dowsing foundation, and have not pushed too hard or too fast, you will receive an accurate response, which we hope would be a comforting "yes." You can then go on with appropriate questioning to locate the missing individual on an unreported shopping trip and be able to answer the caller that Daddy is okay. But we stress that the response must not be preconditioned or forced. It must arise of its own accord, in answer to an appropriate need.

We also want to repeat that if you can avoid falling into fantasy, your dowsing skill will have no limits, except perhaps for the ones you impose on it, and even then, whenever the need arises, the possibility is there to expand your skill. Suppose, for example, that phone call had come at your office and your favorite dowsing device was miles away. The answer may nevertheless unfold in a "knowing" way as it did when you found you didn't need to walk across the field to know where the vein of water was. Perhaps there will then, too, be an instant knowing, and you will find yourself saying, "Oh, Daddy's safe; he just went on a shopping trip and forgot to tell you."

If your mind is now beginning to form the words "deviceless dowsing," we would agree with you; and if you are interested in the scientific pursuit of this aspect of dowsing, you can read the well-written accounts of the research that has been done on it at Stanford Research International in California, under the name of "remote viewing" (see *Mind Reach* by Russell Targ and Harold Puthoff, Delacorte Press, New York, NY, 1977). By deviceless dowsing we do not mean training a part of your body to produce a muscular response or give the feeling of heat or tingling. If you do that, you are turning a part of your body into an extended dowsing device, which is all right, but it would still exhibit all the limitations of an external device. When we use the term deviceless dowsing, we mean the development of a mental "knowing" that can be clearly differentiated from a simple fantasy.

We would point out that dowsing done this way is at least as accurate as that done on-site with a device and contains many more valuable details. The remote and deviceless dowser sees everything at once fully unfolded within his own mind, fully unfolded from that higher level of reality; he sees not only the specific target, but all that it relates to. "Knowing" becomes "seeing" with an inner eye and implies the dowser is now using a different mechanism, a different part of himself, a different degree of resonance of his biosystem and that there has been a changing of gears, so to speak, to a higher range of activity.

We will examine the nature of this different mechanism presently. First, however, let us return to the use of the dowsing tools and suggest ways in which you may practice remote dowsing, or map dowsing, and receive verifiable responses.

10

Map Dowsing

In this chapter you will practice remote dowsing, or map dowsing, from maps of sites that have already been verified, as you did with your on-site dowsing. You'll probably decide to use a pendulum, because most people find that in the long run it is the easiest tool for the job.

Over the next few pages you will find maps of three properties located near Danville, Vermont. Each of them contains a well that was successfully dowsed and then either drilled or dug. On each map you will try to reconstruct the site of the well as it exists now ("now" in this case meaning "at the time the map was drawn and the information verified") and trace the veins of water (called feeder veins) flowing into it, including all relevant information—depth, quality of the water on a 10-point scale, and the minimum year-around flow in gallons per minute. We have arranged these maps into three stages of difficulty, so that you may practice each stage in turn until you achieve answers with confidence and reliability.

THE FIRST STAGE

You will first be working with a map that already shows the location of the well and its feeder veins and includes all other relevant information. Think of it as the map with training wheels. We suggest that you practice on this map until you are able to receive responses that consistently match the information already indicated. We do caution you that there may be other veins or obsolete pipes on the site not related to the well, so don't be surprised if you receive additional responses elsewhere. Those additional responses, which are not the ones we want for our purposes, merely indicate that you need to visualize your target more clearly and rephrase your question, as you may have had to do when you were practicing your on-site dowsing.

It does not matter that the target is already indicated, because at this stage we will accomplish two basic objectives: first, we simply remind ourselves of the coding we have given the pendulum and create an unconscious, automatic response; and second, not so simple, we establish a resonance with the target. That second part is the hardest because in order to establish that resonance we also have to establish that way of thinking about ourselves and the world around us that we have already talked about, and it may not be exactly like the thinking to which we're accustomed. Remember that we are using a model, new to most of us, that says we are *already* in contact with the target, in roughly the way that your radio is already in contact with any particular station whether or not it is tuned to it. Our job, you will recall, is to establish a resonance with the target, which we do by going through the ritual of dowsing.

Your first task with the Site A map (Figure 13), and with each of the later ones, is to develop a dowsing response at a spot that indicates the verifiable location of the well. Before you begin, take a few moments to practice the coding you have already established for the pendulum: clockwise for yes, counterclockwise for no, and an oval for "We're getting there." Then place a straight edge (a ruler or the side of a pencil) along the bottom of the map. While you move your pendulum in the search mode (back and forth) with your dominant hand, use your other hand to move the straight edge slowly up from the bottom of the map. At the same time, visualize, as accurately as you are able, a drilled well with veins of water intersecting it at various depths. Be sure to hold this *idea* of the well site clearly in mind as you ask for its location. Then, as your straight edge approaches the well site, your pendulum should start to move to an oval; and when the straight edge crosses the site of the well, you should get a full clockwise response from your pendulum. If this were an unmarked map, it would mean that the well was located somewhere along the line formed by the straight edge. You verify this

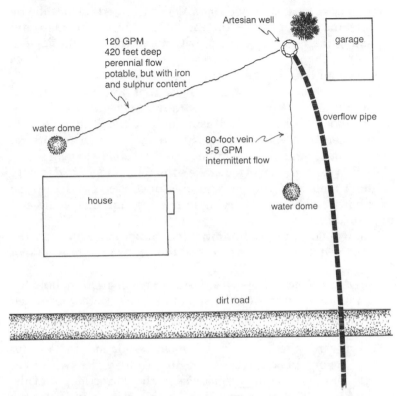

Figure 13. Map of Site A, containing all necessary information about the well. Use this for preliminary practice in map dowsing.

horizontal location by placing the straight edge at the top of the map and repeating the same procedure while you move the edge downward. Once the horizontal line is verified, remember or mark its location.

Next, place the straight edge on the left side of the map. Keeping the idea of the well site clearly in mind, ask for its location as before and, with your pendulum in the search mode, move the straight edge slowly across the map toward the right. Your pendulum should again begin to move to a clockwise oval as you approach the target and then to a full circle when the straight edge crosses the well site. Verify this vertical location by placing the straight edge on the right side of the map and repeating the process as you slowly move the straight edge to the left. If the map were unmarked, the point where the lines cross would indicate the location of the well.

That concludes the first step. Now that you have a "fix," a definite location, the next step is to discover various kinds of information about the well. It is no more difficult than the first step, except that you will be asking questions that require responses at a slightly more subtle level. The ability to gain verifiable answers at this level may take somewhat longer to develop, so don't force it. If you do, you may unconsciously set up the very barriers that you are trying to remove, and this would add to your difficulty.

You will now practice finding three things about the well: the depth, the quality of the water, and the year-round rate of flow.

1. *The depth of the well.* As an aid to your concentration, hold the point of your pencil on the site of the well. With your tuned pendulum in the search mode, ask, "What is the depth of this well from the surface of the ground?" If you then count downward in feet (as you did on site while locating a water pipe), your pendulum will begin to move clockwise near the depth and be fully clockwise at the correct depth. This, the first of the three instructional maps, already indicates the verifiable depth. If you hold this depth in mind for this particular well as you dowse, you will be better able to entrain your mind to the correct response, and that entrainment will become easier in later attempts. Remember that at this stage we are still learning how to establish resonance with the target from a distance, so take your time.

2. *The quality of the water.* Think of the clearest, purest, best-tasting water you can imagine. This would rate a 10 on your scale. At the other extreme, water that is distinctly polluted or unpalatable would be a 1. Generally speaking, dowsers look for a minimum quality of 7 when they are seeking a well site. Again place the point of your pencil on the well in order

to focus your concentration, activate your pendulum, and ask, "What is the quality of the water from this well?" Find it by first counting upward—one, two, three, and so forth—until you get a response. Note the response, and then continue to ten as you observe the precision of that response. Your pendulum should swing in the search mode until you are very close to the appropriate number. Then check that response by counting down from ten. If your answer differs from the one on the map, again remind yourself of the correct response and try again.

3. *The year-round rate of flow.* This is determined in gallons per minute (gpm), and you can use the same procedure that you did above by asking, "What is the minimum year-round rate of flow from this well?" Notice that you seek the minimum flow, not the average, because the well would be inadequate if it produced 10 gpm during the wet season and became dry during the summer. Five gpm would be the minimum flow that you seek, because that flow would be enough to meet the needs of the average family. A flow below 3 gpm in the ground would not really be adequate. Again, start low and count upward, and then check by starting high and counting downward. If your answer differs from the figure on the site map, remind yourself that in this case "now" means when the map was drawn, not when you are doing the dowsing. Go through the procedure again until your results match the ones indicated. Above all, stay relaxed and focused on the task at hand. If you begin to feel tired, quit and try again later.

Now that you have information about the well itself, you will trace the veins feeding into the well. Before you begin, make sure you understand the general procedure, which is the same that you used for on-site dowsing. The well for any of these sites may have more than one feeder vein, but you will be dowsing for only one vein at a time.

Begin by placing the point of your pencil again on the well site and asking how many veins of water feed into it. There may be veins located deeper than the well and running directly under it, but these would not be included. After your pendulum indicates the same number of veins as marked on the map, find the path of the most active vein. In order to do this you activate your pendulum with one hand and, with your other hand, spiral out from the well with your pencil while concentrating on the most active flowing vein of water. Place a dot or an "X" at each location of the spiral to which your pendulum responds. If you then connect those marks, you should have a good approximation of the path of the vein. You *must*, however, remain focused on *that one vein alone* so that you will avoid a response to any other veins.

Next touch the point of your pencil to that vein, hold the idea of the vein again in mind (just as you would if you were on site), and ask for its depth in feet. Find it by counting downward, as you did for the depth of the well, but be clear whether you are asking for the depth of the top of the vein, the center, or the bottom—the site maps indicate the depth to the center of each vein. Determine the quality of the water in that specific vein as you did for the well as a whole, and finally determine the year-round minimum rate of flow.

This same procedure should be followed for determining the second most active vein, and so on. Whenever your answers differ from those indicated on the map, again entrain your mind to the appropriate answers and remember that these are the answers for the time that the site was mapped.

You should follow this same sequence when dowsing all three of these sites: (1) locate the well, (2) discover information about the well, and (3) trace the veins feeding into the well.

While you are doing this practice work, you will reach a stage at which you will begin to wonder, "Is this really happening? Am I really achieving resonance with the target?" The answer is yes, you are. You may not be in complete resonance at the beginning, but as you refine your skill, you soon will be. Once you do convince yourself that you are really doing it, then the skill becomes established, and from then on your job is to refine that skill, like a musician after he discovers how to produce the correct sound from his complex instrument.

THE SECOND STAGE

After you have completed your practice with the first site map, which has all the information already indicated on it, you are ready to remove one set of those training wheels and work with Site B (Figure 14), which shows the location of the well and its

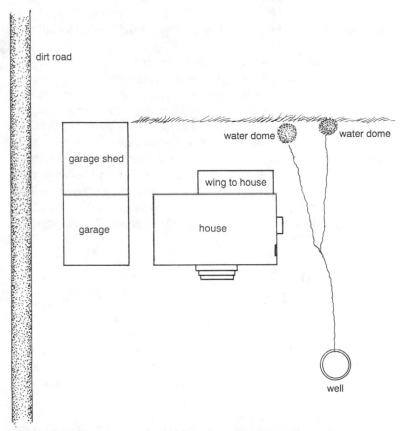

Figure 14. Map of Site B, containing partial information about the well. You should try to determine the depth of the two veins where they join, the year-around flow of water from the well, and the quality of the water.

characteristics but gives no information about the veins. First practice finding the information about the location and characteristics of the well exactly as you did for Site A, using the information that is already given on the map as your guide. This will ensure that you have in mind the appropriate well and that your mind is "tuned" to the right information. Then try to reconstruct the location of the veins flowing into it and discover the other basic information about the water. After you have finished your preliminary work to the best of your ability, check your findings with the completed map, which indicates all the information, in Appendix C.

If your results do not agree with the completed map, try to determine why any errors were made. Were you finding a vein that is nearby but not a part of the well? Perhaps your rational mind tried to create a connection that did not really exist, or perhaps the vein was too deep to flow into the well. Mistakes occur from incorrect assumptions, conscious or unconscious. Everyone makes them, but you should learn to use such mistakes as vehicles for learning: after you determine why any errors were made, retrain yourself with the correct answers. The completed map is available so that you may go through this retraining. Take the time to practice on it before you move on to the third stage.

THE THIRD STAGE

The third map, Site C, shows the house site only, which means that both sets of training wheels are now removed (Figure 15). Your job is to discover the well site, the veins, and three basic facts about each. When you are locating the well, remember to keep the idea of a functioning well in place clearly in mind; when you are locating the veins, hold the idea of a vein of water feeding into that well. This is the same procedure you used for Sites A and B. You will first find the well site, then the information about the well, and finally the location of the feeder veins. If you wish, you may also try to locate the septic system and the path of the water pipe from the well to the house. Remember to take your time; you're still new at this.

After you have found what you believe to be the valid infor-

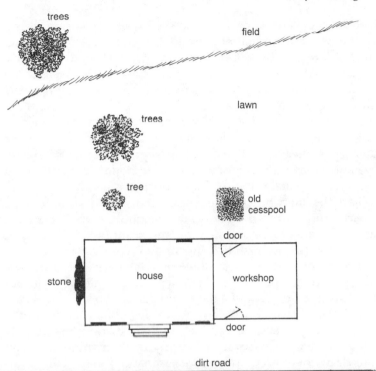

Figure 15. Map of Site C, containing no information about the well. You should try to determine the location of the well and the two veins feeding it, the location of the two water domes feeding the well and their distance, the location and composition of the water line to the house, and the location of the septic tank and leach field.

mation, check your findings with the completed map in Appendix D. Do not expect perfection at this stage. If you did make errors, try again to analyze them, and practice correct responses on the completed map. Only by this constant practice will you increase your rate of success.

THE FOURTH STAGE

Now we come to the final stage, which requires that you have a friend whose water supply is a dowsed well or a spring. It is a step that will bring together map dowsing and on-site dowsing. Before you begin you will need a map of your friend's property that does *not* include any information about the well or its location. On this map try to (1) reconstruct the location of the well and its feeder veins and (2) determine the other essential information as you did at each of the earlier stages. You may, of course, extend this map dowsing so that you also locate the water pipes, the sewer pipes, and the septic system. Use exactly the same procedures for dowsing your friend's map that you have already practiced with the maps in the book.

When the map dowsing is completed, go to your friend's property and do the field dowsing. Begin by standing on the edge of the area to be investigated and scanning, the way you did earlier—that is, first holding one of your L-rods in your hand, arm outstretched, and slowly moving back and forth until you "lock on" to your target. Then try to locate all the contributory veins, the depths and quality and permanence of the flows, and the right place to drill to produce the well. Then go to the various areas you scanned and verify them by dowsing directly on the site. Fix these spots so clearly in your mind that you could draw them accurately on an unmarked map. This information in turn can be checked and verified by your friend. With practice you will find that the "X" you placed on the map while dowsing it before you went to the site will correspond with the location you find while on the site, which will in turn correspond with the verified location and recorded information already in your friend's possession.

Many experienced dowsers do all their preliminary work on maps before going onto a site. They find that doing so saves them time, because the map work is simple, clear-cut, and allows them to have an overview of an entire site at one glance. Accuracy will increase with practice, and continued practice will also increase your confidence. All you have to do is stay focused on the target you are dowsing and remember that yes, you really are doing all this from a map. The next chapter will help make the reason for that "yes" a little more understandable.

11

The Paradigm
and Beyond

We have now completed some of the groundwork that you must master before you can become a good, accomplished dowser. You have practiced developing your dowsing skill through the first three of those seven stages we spoke of earlier: on-site, to-the-horizon, and over-the-horizon. You have also begun to consider a model, or paradigm, for understanding how dowsing works and have placed some of the concepts relating to that model within the context of the leading edge of science.

Now it is time to develop our model for dowsing from another direction, that of the dowser himself. We are not going to be leaving science behind, but we are going to include a bit of material that is presently outside the province of conventional thinking. We start, though, with a comment from a French biologist, Nobel Laureate Charles Richet, who was quoted as saying in 1913, "We must accept dowsing as a fact. It is useless to work experiments merely to prove its existence. It exists. What is needed is its development." (See Christopher Bird, *The Divining Hand*.) The situation today remains very much as it was then, three-quarters of a century ago, except that now we are able to construct a model that potentially may be useful in charting a course for that development.

You may recall the comment we attributed to that sixth dowser earlier in the book. He said, "It works, and as long as it works, I don't care how." We said that dowser had some sort of concept even though he didn't express it, but even so, some students of dowsing may still ask if it is *important* to delve into the rationale of dowsing. After all, some who don't bother can still be good dowsers. And besides, we enjoy our CB radios and our computers without knowing very much about how they work. So is it important to construct this model?

We feel that it is, and we do so for one key reason. If the dowser doesn't have some understanding of his art, he will not know its scope; and if he does not know its scope, his competence and opportunities for service will thus be limited. Our goal is to view dowsing as an art and to develop its everyday usage into a fine craft. If we have a concept of the *how* and *why* of dowsing, we then can realize where we stand—can make at least a rough estimate of our competence and our future potential—and can decide whether or not we are ready to move ahead. The how and why are not easy matters to develop. Just as there is no scientific explanation for what thought is, there is none for what dowsing is, and we are largely on our own. That is why we have been trying to develop a useful paradigm.

STAGES OF DOWSING

If there is a developmental aspect to dowsing, a stage-by-stage growth in it, there must be a basis for the increasing attunement that brings each consecutive success. Thus, we have felt that it would help us to look at dowsing as a sevenfold affair (Table 1): first, locating things on-site; second, finding things accurately to the horizon; and third, finding things over the horizon. These are the three stages we have developed in our instructions and the only ones that can be covered to any extent in this basic book. The fourth stage, as we indicated earlier, ignores space and involves finding abstract and nonphysical targets, often without the use of an external dowsing device, in a totally mental act. It may also ignore time, as in the commonly asked question, "Will this vein of water flow all year?" At the fifth stage you may discover that you are able to cooperate with nature to the extent not only of finding a running underground stream, but of moving it, likewise in a totally mental act. By the sixth stage you might reach the point of such a complete relationship with the target that you can, working through the subtlest of levels, suggest and accomplish the rearrangement of

TABLE 1
The Seven Stages of Dowsing

1. Location of physical targets such as underground flowing water *on site*.

2. Location of physical targets at a distance and *up to the dowser's horizon*.

3. Location of physical targets *over the horizon*.

4. Activity in Steps 1, 2, and 3 in regard to *nonphysical and abstract* problems, often without a device, *in a totally mental act*, including those involving time and other levels of being.

5. *Cooperation with nature*, as in moving underground streams in a totally mental act.

6. *Co-creation with nature*, as in some forms of distant healing of man, animal, and plant.

7. Experience, however brief, of total *conscious union with Creative Forces*—"reflexive" union.

---

forces resulting in changes in our reality as it unfolds from the implicate order. This is the case, for example, in some forms of distant healing. The seventh stage—the ultimate stage—is to attain such attunement with the creative flow that one can live, if only for an instant, within the creative process in what might be called a reflexive mode. This seventh stage is reached neither through training nor through expectation, because it unfolds of its own accord only when the student is ready and, as with each previous stage, has mastered all the stages that come before it and can truly be said to live, move, and have his being consciously, at every moment, within the Creative Order.

You can see from these stages that there is a progression, as there is in any human endeavor; and therefore there must be an apt explanation for how we develop, how we select our field of interest, and how we condition ourselves and expand our awareness. When we reach stages six and seven, we may become spiritual healers, but those who have reached these stages have usually gone through all the previous ones and obtained solid results at each level before they applied themselves to the more exotic challenges of, say, healing at a distance. There is nothing instant in any of this except, perhaps, for that first reaction with the hand-held device.

But we still need to ask what the basis is for this increasing attunement. Dowsing in one form or another has been around since man first walked on the earth. So why haven't we known how it works long before now?

Our answer lies in a question: have we been able to establish a proper model for it, or have we been trying to build our models with an all-too-limited concept?

A MATTER OF RESONANCE

We have constructed our model so far on the basis of some of the suggestions from modern physics and brain-mind studies. Now we will come at it from the other side, tentatively, through answers that dowsing itself can provide, with judgment by results. It is the facts that count here: there must be a bottom line, there must be something we can certify as a result. Unless we can repeatedly produce these results and achieve whatever it is we are seeking, we have simply stopped short of manifesting what we set out to accomplish, we have no hard evidence, and we are indulging in fantasy. However, if we achieve consistent, harmonious results over a long period of time while adhering to the same pattern of dowsing behavior, the chances are that we will be reflecting a major aspect of a true model of the dowsing function. Perhaps by using the dowsing process itself we can elicit some additional details for our model, keeping in mind that all we are seeking at this time is a working model of the dowsing art.

When we turn to dowsing itself to create this working model, we must leave some of our conventional assumptions behind. For example, if we suggest that dowsing ultimately has next to nothing to do with the accepted thinking about the electromagnetic field, much less with the changes that take place in it, we force ourselves to struggle with concepts outside the realm of classic science. Many scientists would hold that dowsing is, if anything, a function of the magnetic gradient—that is, that the dowser reacts to fluctuations in the particular magnetic field of that part of the earth over which he is walking. Experiments connected with this aspect of dowsing have been reported in back issues of *The American Dowser*. At least one scientist who would accept the role of the magnetic gradient, in this case a nuclear physicist noted in his field, when questioned about distant dowsing or map dowsing, simply dismissed it as "psychic" and therefore irrelevant. But how can an open-minded scientist take this position? The fact is that most experienced dowsers *are* remote dowsers, having learned that they can save both time and effort by looking the target over from home or office first. In fact, we offer the premise that once a student becomes a competent dowser, he can tell what is beneath any given square meter on the surface of the globe, once he knows its location.

We suggest that what is at work when we dowse is a *resonance with a creative spin*. Our dowsing indicates to us that the delivery system of all nature, all creation, is a double helix–two oppositely moving corkscrews of force, intertwined, like the caduceus that is the emblem of the medical profession, or like the DNA molecule (which, incidentally, we think is entrained by and is a manifestation of this primal force). This chain of being is always present, everywhere and everywhen, spinning out of what is unmanifest, latent, and innate; in other words, spinning out of the matrix of the universe. The yogis and sufis have given us various descriptions of this simple pattern that we hold is the essence of all things as does the Cabbala. In *The Mystic Spiral*

(Thames and Hudson, London, 1980), author Jill Purce provides us with a diagram of the Cabbala as in Figure 16 and comments in her text as follows:

> The universe, according to the Cabbala, becomes manifest through the materialization of four progressively denser worlds: Aziluth (Archetypal), Briah (Creative), Yetzirah (Formative), Assiah (Material). These worlds, which correspond to those of Plato, are depicted as superimposed trees [Figure 16], in which the lowest Sephira, the Malkuth (kingdom) of each higher world, is the Kether (crown) of the world below. There is always a change of direction between two successive worlds; the contracting vortex, spiralling down to the Malkuth of the Archetypal world, changes direction and starts to expand in its capacity as the Kether of the Creative world.

Such arcane references are encouraging to dowsers who can find four such spirals linked together, surrounding and containing a natural object. Students who are new to dowsing can easily find the double helix enshrouding any plant, bush, or tree as it grows within this conical shape. Subliminal, soundless yet having vibration, and with rates of spin that vary according to the creation of which it is the essential part, this all-pervasive form can be understood by the dowser as nature's creative code, "descending" from the implicate state through "spiritual," "causal," and "astral" densities to the atomic world of materiality. The relevance of such a concept to our model is simply that if every target, material or otherwise, reflects this quadrapartite chain of being, it can be the object of harmonic search and discovery.

In our model the dowser, by phrasing his request, sets up somewhere in his own biosystem a "spin" similar to that of the target, and as he goes through the ritual of scanning or searching, this spin "locks on" to the spin of the target, in phase with it and resonant with it to the point of entraining and activating the pendulum or Y-rod or L-rod he may be holding. The biosystem has already established a harmonic with the target, and the dowsing tools, as an extension of the dowser, attempt to turn or twist in agreement, and so confirm its presence.

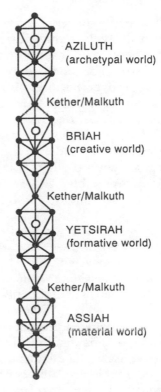

AZILUTH
(archetypal world)

Kether/Malkuth

BRIAH
(creative world)

Kether/Malkuth

YETSIRAH
(formative world)

Kether/Malkuth

ASSIAH
(material world)

Figure 16. The four superimposed, interpenetrating worlds of the Cabbala may be viewed as a descent from the archetypal world (Aziluth), to the creative (Briah), to the formative (Yetsirah), to the material world (Assiah).

Creation in the Cabbala is seen as the vibratory extension of God himself in the form of four superimposed worlds. These are either implicit in a single Tree of Life, or seen as four Trees placed end to end, or in a third relationship, the four worlds are seen as inter-penetrating. . . . As the vibrations are more refined going up through the Trees, the dimensions increase. . . . As the dimension changes, so does the direction. If this world is predominantly right-handed or clockwise, then the world above is anti-clockwise. . . .

Jill Purce, *The Mystic Spiral*, p. 123
(London: Thames and Hudson, 1980).

Should this simple concept be correct, it would explain every one of the seven levels of dowsing activity mentioned earlier. The ability to become in phase with a physical target on-site or near-at-hand would be followed by the ability to become resonant with a target over the horizon and eventually with abstract or intangible targets, which of course are also resonant constructs of the creative spin just described. Resonance, in this view, is the key to a concept. We believe you could do worse, as interested dowsers, than consider this as the basis of a model and concept of what you do when you perform the miracles that dowsing renders possible.

OUR BIOSYSTEM

Let's use this concept and see what we can develop with it. We'll ask where in our biosystem this alleged resonance takes place. First, what *is* the biosystem? Our dowsing device says we are something more than skin and bones, more than molecules and cells and tissue. We will ask *what* more, and our search will take us beyond the recognized limit of our physical selves.

Our dowsing tells us that our biosystem includes bands of a subtle anatomy, each of a distinct quality and rate of vibration, that are separate yet interrelated parts of it. The first band can be dowsed about half an inch from the physical surface of the body, but it can, however, be considered a part of the physical body, rather than extraphysical. The next band is located about four inches beyond the skin surface. Is it physical or is it nonphysical in its provenance? Neither yes nor no to either: it is both, at least as far as we customarily understand those terms and are able to shape them into a question. The limit of the next surround is about eight inches from the surface. Is this to be thought of as extraphysical rather than physical? Yes. The next sheath is around thirteen inches away and is definitely said to be contributing to the physical body rather than the other way around. Finally, at arm's length, we come to the limit of an oval-shaped envelope enclosing the body, head-to-toe, which is even more contributory to the material body and more rarefied in substance according to our dowsing. We also find that if an individual is made the subject of a blessing, especially by a group, the three last-mentioned bands enlarge and extend significantly farther from the body.

When a blessing is given, something is changed. We conventionally think of a blessing as a nonphysical event, but maybe our understanding is too limited. Thoughts, it appears, are things; and with that concept we are that much safer in saying that each of us has, yes, a biosystem not limited to our physical bodies but including an invisible anatomy that is full of life and subject to change according to the thoughts and moods that are created. But now back to our earlier question: can we determine the seat of the resonance that we proposed as the key to what we call dowsing? We find, again by our dowsing, that the site of the model wave created by this resonance is in the region of the so-called third eye, opposite the pineal gland, a few inches from the forehead. When we begin the process of dowsing and ask a question while we hold an image in mind, the spin-model is there; when we dismiss the question and release the image, the spin-model vanishes.

You can test these suggestions—for that's all they are—as you proceed in your dowsing career. We hope they may be helpful. There is historical precedence for the rings of the biosystem we've found, even if there is none for the presence of the spin model that we said our dowsing quest established, although there are fascinating hints for that, too, in the drawings and descriptions in primitive cultures of the invisible "magician's crest," extending from the mid-brow.

THE INVISIBLE ANATOMY

We now turn to an overview of the search for this invisible anatomy of the body. None of what we say can presently be substantiated by academic science, just as none of the sheaths we have mentioned can be, at least not until electronic instruments of sufficient subtlety are available to give dial-and-needle confirmation of what the dowsing device says is there. [An account of the twentieth-century search for the invisible anatomy can be found in David Tansley's insightful book, *The Raiment of Light* (Routledge & Kegan Paul, London, 1984).]

In the Vedas of ancient India, and from the time of Hippocrates in the fifth century B.C., there are references to the Vital Body and the *augoeides*, or light sheaths, surrounding the human form. The idea of a vital force animating the physical body was a firmly held belief in the eras of Galen and Paracelsus, and the notion of an elixir of life remained as a frame of reference for all physicians and researchers until the nineteenth century when, as we previously noted, electricity and magnetism became the watchwords of a burgeoning science. Interest in the aura and the vital force waned as material science then waxed, and those who kept it alive were considered hopelessly dated and "unscientific."

They nevertheless persisted. In 1905 Annie Besant and Bishop Leadbetter wrote a book, *Thought-Forms* (Theosophical Publishing House, Wheaton, IL, 1986), that contained detailed descriptions and color plates of their conception of the aura. In 1908 the British physician Dr. Walter Kilner, while practicing at St. Thomas Hospital in London, discovered and developed a process for making the aura visible—apart, as he said, from all occultism. Working with the coal-tar derivative dicyanin applied to a glass screen, he began to view the aura with the naked eye, dividing it into four layers—not five as we have done—and correlating its shape and coloring with various conditions of health. Symmetry, for instance, was the hallmark of a healthy person; asymmetry was not. He recognized that his methods left much to be desired, but he set others on the path, including a Cambridge biologist named Bagnall, who devised a more efficient screen using the derivative pinacyanol.

Other and more recent researchers, Dr. John Pierrakos in New York and Dr. Shafica Karagulla, author of *Breakthrough to Creativity* (Marina Del Rey, CA, De Vorss, 1967), pursued the research using clairvoyance, as we used dowsing earlier. They discovered that any imbalance in the physical body appeared first in the etheric body before it became clinically identifiable as a disease. Dr. Brugh Joy, author of *Joy's Way* (Los Angeles, J. P. Tarcher, 1979), wrote about his far-reaching transformation in becoming suddenly aware of the subtle bodies and their interrelationship.

We must also mention the work done by the brilliant and

thorough Dr. Guyon Richards in England in the 1920s. He incorporated dowsing as a diagnostic tool, but soon devised a method of registering the electrical resistance of the aura in terms of ohms. He would place his subject on a grounded metal plate charged with sufficiently high voltage to light a neon lamp held in the subject's aura by an observer. As the lamp was moved away from the body, it would go out at the limit of one band after another. Thus he measured the extent and intensity of the bodily surrounds, categorizing them as "biomorphs." As we did earlier, he found four-ring and five-ring biomorphs in man, three and four in mammals, three in insects and reptiles, two in vegetables, and one in minerals. Dr. Richards' book, *The Chain of Life* (Essex, The C. W. Daniel Company, 1954), is replete with technical and philosophical conclusions about what we have referred to as the biosystem.

The science we were taught in school was concerned with two fixed ideas. One is embodied in the laws of thermodynamics, which hold that the universe is a closed system and that within this enclosure energy can only dissipate and never be renewed. These laws say that there is no source of renewal. The second fixed idea is akin to the first and has to do with local causality. It holds that nothing can happen without an immediate cause in time and space; there can be no domino effect from an undetermined "somewhere else."

Needless to say, these views of reality worked very well in the materialistic world of the nineteenth and twentieth centuries and permitted the development of much of our industry and commerce, but with the arrival of quantum theory, the old certainties began to give way, and today it is a brand new ball game. In 1935 a closet dowser named Einstein (yes, that's right; see *The American Dowser*, 20:2, May 1980) set out to prove that the statistical predictions of particle behavior set forth by quantum theory implied that twin particles behaved the same way at the same time, even though they might be situated at opposite ends of the universe—an impossibility in the view of physicists because there could be no communication faster than the known speed of light, and no infraction of the principle of local causality. Einstein simply wanted to make the point that quantum theory was incomplete, and that there had to be a more inclusive and conclusive structure to material existence. In 1965 J. S. Bell set out to prove quantum theory to be correct but, in the process, confirmed Einstein's *reductio*; and in 1972 John Clauser, with a complicated apparatus in his lab at Berkeley, further supported Einstein's contention by producing physical proof that identical particles would react in the same way simultaneously, if a change developed in either one of them.

Physicists were thus compelled to face the issue of simultaneity and perhaps were not overjoyed to do so, but to us investigating a new model for dowsing, the new physics was beginning to make sense, for identical behavior in separated particles can imply a superior and governing common source, and we are back to the implicate order and the creative spin that we postulated as the essence of all that is—the double helix that we suggested was at the center of everything we dowsed for, and for which we created a model in our aura.

A SIMPLE EXPERIMENT

We previously set forth the idea that dowsing may fit in with the new science, and we then suggested how and where it may do so. Let's now, however, approach the subject from the point of view of a simple dowsing experiment, one that you may try with a friend.

Here you are, engaged in an ordinary dowsing experience, dowsing tool in hand, looking for a vein of water, so many feet deep, flowing at a given gpm, minerally balanced and unpolluted. Your friend comes with his dowsing tool and asks, "Is there a model wave-form corresponding to such a target—a standing wave that has been generated by this question and the mental focus?" Yes. "Please locate where it is." He searches and finds it about ten inches in front of the mid-brow. Now you dismiss the search for your target. "Is the standing wave gone?" Yes. "Are the resonance with the target and the precision of the question a function of one another?" Yes. "Is this why we must ask for exactly what we want in order to find it?" Yes, it is the precise question that produces the precise resonance, which then produces the precise results. As should be clear, the precision of the question is critical to the precision of the dowsing response.

PARALLEL WORLDS

In developing our model, we have used the term resonance, and we have attempted to relate it to the findings of the new physics. Our simple formula concerning resonance has not exactly subverted any of the scientific tenets, but we have been leading up to something else. We turn now to a consideration of a subject that may further support the concept that mental resonance is at the heart of dowsing: the subject of parallel worlds. If it is true that science will have little time for the human aura, at least until someone devises an electronic scanner to replace psychic perception or dowsing, it is doubly true in the case of parallel worlds.

We will start with an anecdote. In Venezuela, in the hinterland, one can still come across the red-tiled *haciendas* that were built 400 years ago. One of your authors and his wife were working at one such ranch house when they became aware of an unusual atmosphere. "Hay penas aqui?" he asked his host at a suitable moment. "Pena" is the slang word for phantasma, or ghost. "Yes," came the reply, "I have heard it, but others in the household have seen and even touched it." (He mentioned one such visitor, but your author had become aware of two.)

"It is a misplaced person," the host said, which exactly sums up a suggestion of ours, that such presences cannot be explained away as "thought forms" or mental constructs of a lower order but are, as some of the literature calls them, trapped souls, or those who have failed to make a full transition at death.

The *Journal of the British Society of Dowsers* (Vol. 30:206, December 1984) carried a brief article written with the permission of a woman in a western state whose house had become increasingly difficult to occupy until, in desperation after having *seen* the unwanted visitor, she requested and received relief in the form of intercession offered by one of your authors. In another case the same service was performed for a large, automated industrial plant at the request of its general manager. Following that service, employee dissatisfaction and production difficulties disappeared. Much can be written on this subject, which is barely mentioned here as one of the skills attainable by dowsers who have progressed along the sevenfold path we outlined at the opening of this chapter.

Although many other examples exist in our experience and that of other dowsers, we are not gurus or priests and do not claim any special insights beyond those derived from the dowsing art itself, coupled with an appropriate dowsing model; however, the pattern of misplaced souls is one that is real enough and should not be overlooked. We do wish to stress most strongly, however, that in dowsing one opens oneself to unfamiliar forces, and it is well to be on guard and to master each stage of dowsing thoroughly before moving on to the next. In *Venture Inward* (New York, Harper & Row, 1964), author Hugh Lynn Cayce describes the case of an obsession by a discarnate that had been invited. The outcome was nearly fatal. Although the noxious being was ultimately vanquished, the shock and the warning remained.

Our Bible is a forgotten manual on the subject. The Old Testament inveighs against summoning spirits that "peep and mutter"; the New Testament, in account after account, relates the correlation of spirit invasion and disease. "That kind comes not out," the Master warns his disciples, "except by prayer and fasting." Raise yourself to the necessary level of competence, He was saying, before you undertake an exorcism of that difficulty.

Today little is written or said on the subject of the spirit world, but it is a valid one and it can be dangerous. We look with growing concern at those well-meaning people who innocently seek out spirit guides without discrimination, for those who rely on such contact for their development may do so at their own peril. It is a vast subject, having much to do with the confusion in the world and its current plight, and we can close these comments with no better words than those of the Apostle who said that we wrestle not against the flesh but against principalities and powers, and who advised us to put on the whole armor of light.

TOWARD THE FUTURE

All of this brings us now to a consideration of what the future may hold for what we call dowsing and to the suggestion of a basic philosophy commensurate with that future.

We see the main function of dowsing as a vehicle for the raising of consciousness of all whom it touches. But each step along the way requires that the dowser reach verifiable stages of mastery. Only in this manner can there be true progress, and a central theme of this book has been the idea that progress must go hand-in-hand with proficiency. We seek to develop know-how and, beyond that, an overview of what dowsing may be all about. We need a competence in order to share it with others, and to gain that competence we need a concept of what we have set out to develop. Once we are buttressed as much as possible by a solid judgment based on the results we achieve, we then need to explore the biosystem that we've outlined to you. We need to map its ordinary limits and its changeableness under the many varied conditions of dowsing. We need to discover all we can, both quantitatively and qualitatively; we need to know, insofar as it is safe and practicable, how it relates to our findings in the parallel worlds; we need to know more about the invisible organs and *nadis*, those connecting threads of energy flows, it contains. What we see slowly emerging is a new model of the universe and of humanity's relationship to it, a new capacity to seek, to know, and to serve.

Philosophically, the proposal of Father Teilhard de Chardin (*The Future of Man*, Harper & Row, New York, 1964) to the effect that the earth has a "noosphere" or aura of its own to which we contribute by thought, word, and deed is very appealing. Perhaps the resonant cavity of our planet is an outward, material manifestation of this noosphere of planetary consciousness, one to which we can attune ourselves through meditation and dowsing, and by which we then place our thoughts, words, and deeds in resonance with the more subtle body of the earth itself. After much centered thought, many creative words, and many positive deeds have been put into the noosphere, a critical point must be reached beyond which an overflow, an outflow, occurs, manifesting in the material realm. Such a process feeds on itself, the noosphere holding inspiration for those seekers whose resonant development allows them to bring it to their conscious awareness, enabling them to grow, and in turn to deposit their own constructive concepts for the use of those who come after. This we take to be the meaning of the New Age and the origin of hope for all mankind.

But whether one sees a necessary descent from the spiritual or ideal, to the mental or formative, to the astral or experiential, and finally to the material world, in a fourfold chain of life, it is nevertheless the results that count—the achievement of serviceable effects for one's fellow beings. No spiritual idea is valid without its manifestation. There must be concrete expression in the workaday world. The helical spin we talked about is continuous, deriving from the innate, developing through definite stages, and collecting matter on its way to our denser world. It is all one chain of being, not, we believe, past knowing, and a key to our safety and service in the here and now.

12

Dowsing and Healing

We have said that dowsing is a progressive art and that as we comprehend and master each successive stage, we become ready to move to the next one. If we are correct in what we say, and if our dowsing, when properly developed, leads us from the tangible to the intangible, and beyond that to what we loosely call the implicate, or the spiritual, it then follows that we may eventually develop a resonance so precise that it can result in communication on levels that lead to healing.

Our comments must necessarily be brief. This is merely a cautionary introduction to healing, one of the many areas to which we think dowsing can apply, and nothing more. It is an attractive area to beginners, and many people would like to become healers, but it is also one in which a would-be healer may unwittingly cause harm. In the larger context all elements of creation are interwoven, not only on the material level but on each of the subtle levels of the fourfold waveform. Invasive interference at any level can and does affect not only every aspect of that one level but all other levels as well, and any attempt to heal without due preparation can be self-defeating. We would suggest that if you become ill and someone says, "I'm a healer; I'll fix you up," you should avoid that person's ministrations. Even though he or she might be able to make you feel somewhat better, that feeling may have nothing to do with true healing. In fact, you may want to adopt the following rule of thumb: if a person *says* he is a healer, he is probably not a healer. A dowser, with patience and practice, may advance to the level within which true healing can be accomplished, but to do so successfully he must master each successive stage of the art and develop trust in his ability to act in harmony with the essential forces of nature. In order to reach such a level, he must subdue what may be his own worst enemy, himself, and no dowser who has reached that eminence ever thinks of himself as a healer. He may, from time to time, act in harmony with nature to help effect healing, but he feels no need or desire for self-promotion. His ability arises as an inevitable side effect of his development as a dowser. Each stage of his development brings him into a more precise degree of resonance with all levels of the natural world, and the ability to heal is one of the results of this gradually unfolding process.

If you find that the ability to effect healing does arise as you progress, we ask you to consider several things before you put it to use. The first is to consider that there are, and quite properly so, laws that govern the healing art. There are fifty states and fifty Medical Practice Acts, differing somewhat in each jurisdiction. For example, the State of Vermont, in which the American Society of Dowsers is incorporated, forbids healing and diagnosis *of any kind* except by licensed personnel, with the sole exception of healing done under the auspices of a recognized church. Basically, the laws of each state are designed to eliminate fraud and to protect what the respective legislatures conceive of as legitimate practice. Even though these laws may sometimes seem unfair to would-be healers, they do help to keep meddlers from interfering in other people's lives.

In addition to the fifty state laws, the Pure Food, Drug and Cosmetic Act, passed by the U.S. Congress, makes it a felony to use a device to diagnose or heal, and that includes the use of a dowsing rod or pendulum. Again, the laws may at first glance seem unfair, and may prohibit the use of devices that really do promote diagnosis or healing in a manner unrecognized by conventional science or medicine, but there is also a long history of devices that are at best worthless. With this background, and because of the interest in healing that accompanied the increased prowess of their fellow-members, the Trustees of ASD issued a Statement of Policy defining its position as a corporation articled under the laws of Vermont. We offer this statement for two reasons: first, it is an indication of the seriousness and the sense of obligation taken by responsible dowsers when faced with the legal issues of healing; and second, it is a guideline for anyone seriously contemplating his own development as a healer. It is divided into seven parts. The first part, the "whereas" part, sets the scene, and the proscriptions in the other six parts stem from it.

Part 1. Whereas Authority for the existence and incorporation of ASD flows from its Articles of Association granted by the State of Vermont, which articles cannot and do not authorize legally as a corporate purpose the practice of diagnosis or healing or their promotion or sponsorship; and whereas under Vermont Statute "Medicine and Surgery," Chapter 23, T, 26 Sec. 1311–12 and 1314, anyone who practices medicine *"by any system or method"* (italics added), including those of "faith cure," "laying on of hands" and "mind Healing" (excepting practice of the religious tenets of one's church), "shall be deemed a physician or practitioner of medicine or surgery" and shall require licensing by the State of Vermont, or be subject to prosecution, the following policy has been adopted by your Board of Trustees.

Part 2. Members of the Society wishing to diagnose or heal are notified they do so not as members of ASD, but personally, and at their own risk, and subject to the interpretation of the laws of their own State and the Pure Food, Drug and Cosmetic Act, passed by the U.S. Congress, which makes it a felony to diagnose or heal without a license, and with interstate use of an instrument or device.

Part 3. Defense against prosecution by a State or the Federal Government could be a consuming costly affair, and members cannot be entitled to legal or financial support from ASD for what may be an illegal act.

Part 4. Members who wish to write or talk on bodily diagnosis or treatment, on the other hand, are entitled to do so under the First Amendment to the U.S. Constitution, which guarantees them freedom of speech; in view of ASD's position, however, they may not hold themselves out, in so doing, as representing ASD in any way, but rather as presenting a personal position.

Part 5. Requests coming from a licensed medical doctor in this country should be considered in the context of applicable law, and at the member's own risk. It is pointed out that requests originating with a doctor outside the country, who is not duly licensed in the U.S., constitute such a risk.

Part 6. The question of the legality of discussion or treatment of radiation detrimental to health turns on whether one is holding oneself out as curing disease; it is noted that it would be attempted by a prosecuting attorney to show that this was done by a system or method that was prohibited.

Part 7. Your trustees have directed the ASD staff to reject all requests of a medical nature, either directly or for referral to a member or a chapter, noting to the petitioner that such requests may not be processed under the society's interpretation of the terms of state and federal law.

Please note that the effect of this statement is simply to disclaim corporate sponsorship on the part of ASD of what might be construed as illegal activity. The statement does not prevent individuals from talking about healing or attempting to heal on their own responsibility. It does call attention to the risks involved, with the motivation and hope that all individuals avoid trouble through overzealousness or innocent infractions of current attitudes as expressed in statutes of the fifty states and the federal government.

As we have said, there does seem to be substantial evidence that dowsing, on a certain level and with certain purity of motive, can affect healing. If we consider dowsing as an art, and healing as just one of its expressions and applications, we may well conclude that the art lies in the locating of targets, while that segment of the art called healing manifests through *interaction* with them. We will not go into the pros and cons of expressing this particular power as reach of the mind, but we would suggest seven points, or steps, to those readers interested in the healing mode of dowsing.

The *first* item is that first things come first. There is a step-by-step progress in the art, a competence-in-series to be mastered, before requests for healing can properly be called a part of one's repertoire. Even if the concept held by the dowser is completely harmonious with the intent of healing, it is meaningless unless it is coupled with a verifiable progression of results. We hold that you cannot begin even to consider such a thing as healing until you can, for instance, accurately locate a target at a distance, that is, dowse over-the-horizon or map-dowse.

Second is the point that not only does the dowsing art need to be understood as applying to all seven distinct levels of activity we previously outlined, beginning with on-site dowsing, but the human biosystem also contains, as we have suggested, at least five bands of varying frequencies, each one of which must be understood as being the subject of certain appropriate but unique resonances or contacts that the dowser discovers as he progresses toward the more advanced levels of dowsing.

Third, and this is completely aside from legal considerations, the would-be healer must work with the highest ethics, which is another way of saying he must work within the greatest possible degree of resonance. If he does not, he simply becomes an arrogant trespasser, certain to fail as he encroaches upon another person's condition and sets up disharmony instead of harmony.

Fourth, taking our cue from ancient records, the would-be healer must be safely at home with the concept and patterns of the parallel or overlapping worlds. He must understand them as one part of the totality within which he is working and must be able to deal in a harmonious manner with what is found there.

Fifth, the individual must complete an apprenticeship. We would suggest that until one has received 500, or better yet 1000, anecdotal reports of recoveries from a wide spectrum of acute and chronic disease, including the major killers, the healer will be an apprentice. He must recognize that his failures as well as his successes are a part of that apprenticeship, and that each failure offers him an opportunity to learn and to grow. Only after that apprenticeship is completed will one know that one knows, and be able to discriminate and respond to a valid need.

Sixth, the individual must realize that the art of the healer lies basically in helping others to free themselves from their own conscious or unconscious viewpoints of guilt and self-denigration, so that they can align themselves to their *own* unfailing source of renewal and balance, which may well differ from the one adopted by the healer. The healer must balance his increasing authority with increasing humility, knowing that even though he aids this process, he never overrides it or interferes with the other's free will.

Seventh, we would add that our hypothetical healer also looks for and eliminates external interferences, the so-called obsessions and noxious zones, even if they seem to exist only as memories of conditions as far in the past as childhood and the prenatal period. The dowser-healer must realize that any thought or condition, once established, takes on a life and pervasiveness of its own and acts in an eternal present. It should therefore be obvious that to eliminate any preestablished condition or obsession, that dowser-healer must be able to operate at any distance, to ignore space-time, and to select and communicate on "astral" and "causal" levels at will.

By the time these seven points are mastered and the apprenticeship completed, the dowser who chooses to master the healing mode will know the truth of the saying that "He who claims does not know, and he who knows does not claim."

Epilogue

We now reach the conclusion to this introduction to the art and craft of dowsing. As in the dowsing schools that preceded this book, we have introduced the basic skill of dowsing to you, the reader, by means of a graduated series of practical, verifiable exercises. More critically, however, we have developed these exercises step by step within a constantly evolving paradigm so that you could gradually see how they fit into an increasingly larger context. We told you about the *reach* of dowsing and presented three preliminary stages of a seven-stage progression: on-site, then up-to-the-horizon, and then over-the-horizon. We moved from the material—the location of a pipe or a vein of water—to the abstract—the relative quality of that water or the location of a field of resonance in our bio-system. Corresponding to this, we practiced using the three dowsing tools, found a progression in their use, and suggested that we might ultimately cease to use them. Along the way we developed, with cautions, a model of a way of looking at dowsing that can help us gain confidence and understanding.

If you continue to practice and perfect your dowsing at each preliminary stage and seek to understand the model we have presented, you will develop a grounding that will enable you to move ahead to those progressively more advanced stages of dowsing that lie open to you. As you move toward them, remind yourself that in the long process of foundation building you need to master your skill with each type of target at each stage before moving ahead to the next stage. We all develop our skill that way, because that progress of development allows us to get constant verification, and we are then able to build our confidence as we receive that feedback. It is judgment by con-

crete result, not by abstract concept, but we allow our concept to
enlarge so that those results may occur. One result is that even
though we are still in the world we always knew, we are now
able to view it in a way that is more complete and satisfying than
a more limited concept would have permitted.

Your vision will continue to unfold to the extent that you
allow it to do so. You will, of course, make mistakes as you
continue to learn—every dowser does—and it is important to
look at those mistakes when they happen and try to understand
why they happened. Were you unconsciously programming
yourself for one particular answer? Was your question vague or
not really the one you should have been asking? Did your
attention stray from the job at hand? And, most difficult of all
for many, did you really have the permission and the authority
to seek an answer at that particular time?

That last question is as important as any other topic we have
covered, because the asking of it allows us to move ahead to a
higher level of ethics. For dowsers the code of ethics starts with
those six statements mentioned earlier, but if the idea of service
through dowsing is to take root, that code of ethics must be
continually examined and nurtured from within so that it does
not become compromised by the little "I."

A high level of ethics is also important for reasons that go
beyond the personal self, no matter what the stage of development of that self may be. When you do begin to open yourself to
increasingly subtle levels of information, you will eventually
realize that you are more than simply a receiver of that information. The vast, complex antenna system that is part of you is also
a transmitter, and every thought, attitude, and emotion you
hold radiates outward, creating an effect on every person and
object of your dowsing. You must therefore recognize and accept the responsibility to ask what it is you are transmitting. Is it
an attitude of harmony, is it an achievement of balance, is it an
awareness of a greater good? This is where the asking of permission becomes particularly important, because our dowsing at-
tunes us to the more subtle levels of reality; and if we fail to
dowse from a conviction of service and an attitude of harmony,
we will transmit all the conscious or unconscious disharmony
that lies within us.

THE THREEFOLD PERMISSIONS

Remember that whenever we dowse, we enter someone else's private space. That space can be his personal self, his property, or the land of which he is custodian. Before we invade these private spaces, we must follow a sequence of permissions. First we must be *asked* to dowse; or, if we instigate it, we must at least receive that person's permission to do so. In addition, we must also be certain that we have permission to dowse from what we conceive as the Source of the Highest Good, so that we may help to create or maintain harmony in that space. We dowse for that permission with a threefold question: (1) *May I* seek this information—that is, am I permitted? Good intentions are never enough; and narrow, limited reasoning ahead of time may be inadequate for the dowsing task. (2) *Can I* receive a clear answer that will allow me to be of service—am I able, do I have the skill? Mastery at one level of dowsing does no confer mastery at any other level, no matter how eager we are for that mastery. (3) *Should I* seek it—is it the time and am I the one to do it? It might be that a particular kind of dowsing is inadvisable for you to do at that particular moment and that your well-meant efforts would cause unwitting harm.

We must also realize that there are some situations which are intended to stay as they are for reasons beyond our understanding or awareness. The situation that we observe and label as bad may be there to prevent a worse situation somewhere else, or what we perceive as, say, a sickness or emotional upset may be part of a necessary "toughening-up" for the individual involved. By dowsing for permission, we ask for that awareness, even though we may not understand why that situation must remain, and we must learn to trust the permissions. We are, in turn, entrusted with information about the nature of dowsing and its progressive uses only after we have earned that trust. Knowledge is power, and to know the method of gaining all-knowledge and using that knowledge not only increases our responsibility, but it tests our ability to avoid allowing the little "I" to become enraptured by the sense of personal power. We live in a wavelike continuum that we can traverse only to the extent of our awareness of it, and we can all too easily think our awareness is much greater than it really is. There are risks involved in our journey within it, and a general feeling of good will is not always sufficient for our needs. We are all limited beings, but we must respect those limitations and take the time to allow the necessary capacity to develop.

As we conclude, we hope that whenever you go back through this book, you will continue to find information and techniques that appeal to you, interest you, and support and strengthen you as your personal goals and potentials continue to develop. Our view is that there is one universe, which implies one structure for it and ultimately one set of rules. How we see those rules, how we approach and interpret them, how we are able to identify with them are individual concerns. We hold that these concerns are the essential matter and substance of our dowsing. No matter where each of us starts from, we all approach the same path, but each one of us must ultimately find his own way toward that path. We are, of course, pleased with any contribution we may have made toward giving a shape and substance to the teaching and the learning of dowsing, and we hope that you will be able to continue the journey forward and in the process add your contribution to that shape and substance.

We are all still beginners, and the road ahead extends beyond our present range of vision. As sincere dowsers we wish you the joy of the journey as we have experienced it, and we express to you our thanks for this encounter on the path.

APPENDICES

Appendix A

Tools for Dowsing

Various small companies manufacture dowsing (or "divining") tools for prices that vary from a few dollars to several hundred dollars. There is no harm in purchasing and using these tools, if they suit your fancy, but none of them will make you a better dowser. We hold that any tool can be the "best" one for you, and for many dowsers this means that the best tool is the one you make yourself—not because it will have any magical qualities, but simply because it is the cheapest and most satisfying way to acquire a complete set of dowsing tools. You can purchase the basic components for under a dollar and be all set up in less than an hour. How well you dowse with them is then up to you, not up to the fanciness of the equipment. If you are averse to assembling them, the next best step is to purchase them at reasonable cost from the American Society of Dowsers, Danville, VT 05828. All three devices will then cost you slightly under twenty dollars, but in exchange you will receive good, sturdy tools that will last indefinitely.

Here are suggestions for making your own tools.

THE L-RODS

The least expensive L-rods can be made with two wire coat hangers and two plastic soda straws. You will also need a pair of pliers, a wire cutter, and scissors. Cut the coat hangers near one side of the crosspiece and near the hook, as shown below. Then straighten each wire and hold it in your closed fist so that about

115

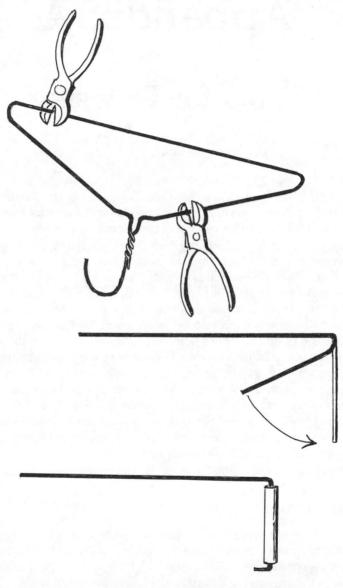

Figure 17. Steps in making an L-rod. (1) Cut a wire coat hanger as shown, (2) bend the wire sharply at right angles, (3) insert into a plastic sleeve and bend the wire underneath the sleeve.

an inch of the wire projects below your fist (Figure 17). About a half inch above your fist, bend the wire sharply to form an L.

Next, hold the plastic soda straw in your closed hand and cut it so that a small portion projects beyond each side of your fist. You then slide this onto the short part of the wire and then bend the end of the wire with a pair of pliers so that the straw will not slide off. Do the same with the other plastic soda straw and wire, and you have your set of L-rods.

If you have the tools, you can also use two $3/16$-inch metal rods about 18–24 inches long. You would bend them about 6 inches from the end and slide on loose plastic or metal tubing, likewise bending the end of each handle so that the tubing stays on but still moves freely. If you order from ASD, that is the kind of L-rod you will receive.

THE Y-ROD

The least expensive Y-rod costs nothing, and all you need is a sharp knife—even a jackknife will do. You find a tree with sturdy but flexible branches, like a fruit tree. Your Y-rod should have two branches, each about 18–24 inches long, that are about equal in thickness and relatively easy to move, joined at a butt cut to about 4 inches (Figure 18).

Many dowsers now use Y-rods made from $1/4$- to $3/16$-inch plastic tubing or glass-reinforced plastic rods. They join them together with a little glue and an electrical cap or sturdy cord. The main requiremint of a Y-rod is that it be flexible but require some tension to be held in the search position. ASD carries Y-rods of various lengths made from both plastic tubing and glass-reinforced rods. The ones 18 or 24 inches long are the most popular and are the easiest for the beginner to use.

THE PENDULUM

A pendulum is nothing more than a centered weight attached to a string or chain, and a hex nut attached to a 1-foot length of sewing thread works well at minimal cost. It is not a perfectly centered weight, but it will serve well as a training device. Some

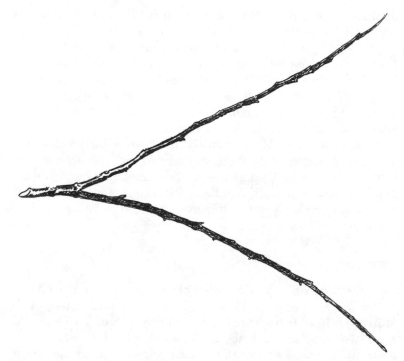

Figure 18. The Y-rod, or forked stick, cut from a tree.

experienced dowsers become so used to it that they prefer it to anything else.

An alternative, likewise inexpensive, is a $1^1/_2$-inch wooden ball, with a small "eye," as is used in picture framing, screwed into it. The thread then attaches to the eye.

ASD and its British counterpart, BSD, both stock well-centered metal pendulums, either teardrop or bullet shaped, which are the kind most dowsers end up using.

Appendix B

Record Keeping

We do need a certain structure in our dowsing endeavors, no matter what our degree of experience. Each dowser develops different interests, and you will find that those interests you develop will govern the records you devise. These records serve both you and your clients. Here are some suggestions for keeping a record of each of your water-dowsing ventures.

For whom dowsed:

Address:

PREDICTION

Date dowsed:

Site (or sites) staked or otherwise marked —
Description (number of veins feeding that site, both horizontally
   and vertically, and whence they come) —
Depth to top of vein(s) (different levels) —
Depth to bottom of vein(s) (different levels) —
Width of vein(s) —
Pressure (scale of 1–10) —
Quality of water in vein(s) (potability, purity) —
Durability of flow (year-round?) —
Hardness of water —
Temperature of water —
Nitrates (ppm) —

Nitrites (ppm) —
pH of water —
Remarks (clay, sand, boulders, etc.) —

RESULTS

Date drilled:

Flow encountered (at different levels, and total) —
Remarks (Drilled as sited? Speed of drill? Diversion attempts?
   Explosives or CO_2 used? Attitude of driller? etc.) —

The sample above is one that you might need for water, but the objects of your search are limitless, as many as your mind can relate to; for the sake of your progress as a dowser, remember that the befores and afters are your true teachers. Take time to note them down and keep them in order, so that when the phone rings or the letter comes, you can refer to them without delay.

The greatest record you can compile, however, is the one of service. That is where your efforts count and where your reward is.

Appendix C

Completed Map
of Site B

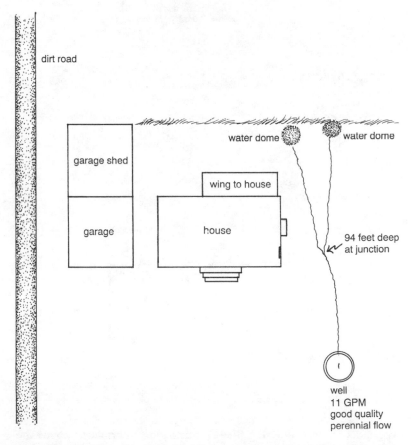

dirt road

water dome   water dome

garage shed

wing to house

garage   house

94 feet deep
at junction

well
11 GPM
good quality
perennial flow

Appendix C. Map dowsing Site B, containing information about the
well. Use this as reference for further practice with the earlier site map.

Appendix D

Completed Map
of Site C

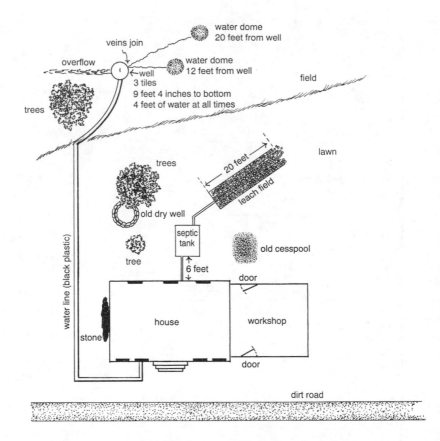

Appendix D. Map dowsing Site C, containing information about the well, water line, and septic system. Use this as reference for further practice with the earlier site map.

Appendix E

Experimental Accounts

Examples of the reach of the divining mind abound within the pages of *The American Dowser*, published by the American Society of Dowsers, Inc., Danville, VT 05828. This quarterly journal began as a mimeographed publication in 1961 and is now an award-winning, digest-sized magazine sent to members in 42 countries.

Experiential accounts are, however, not limited to the publications of the American Society of Dowsers. For the English reader the *Journal of the British Society of Dowsers* (Hastingleigh, Ashford, Kent, England TN25 5HW) is another well-edited source of anecdotal record.

In addition, other smaller newsletters contain such accounts. Two columns, written by one of your authors and pertinent to the material touched upon, are included here. The first deals with the topic of geopathogenic stress that has been the subject of scientific research funded by the Federal Republic of Germany. It is from the June 1989 *Newsletter of the West Midland Dowsers* (25 Calthorpe Close, Walsall, England WS5 3LT), an independent dowsing group associated with the British Society of Dowsers. The second, which connects historical examination of the dowsing mode with modern findings, is from the Fall 1988 issue of *The Canadian Dowser*, the publication of the Canadian Society of Dowsers, c/o Robert Brewer, Box 129, Beeton, Ontario, Canada LOG 1AO. Both are bimonthly newsletters.

TERRY ROSS'S COLUMN, *NEWSLETTER*
***OF THE WEST MIDLAND DOWSERS*, JUNE 1989**

Geopathogenic zones, noxious zones, irritation zones—how

123

long will they remain unsolved mysteries? I offer three anecdotal accounts from which the reader may derive an opinion.

Gordon MacLean was the grand old man and president of the American Society of Dowsers from 1967 to 1969. I recall him visiting the then new headquarters of the Society, full of concern that the three staff members who worked there be free from exposure to noxious zones. After whipping out the large Y-rod he used, he promptly located three shallow veins flowing beneath the office floor. He was puzzled. There was something different about his dowsing reaction. "Somebody," he announced, "has done something to these veins. They're okay." Somebody had. Somebody had mentally imprinted a benign modality on each and every one of them, a modality that remains in force today, rendering them nonnoxious, safe, and, as Gordon found them, "okay." Perhaps you can give them a long-distance dowse.

The second anecdote came in the form of a panic phone call from one who had suffered the effects of the Epstein-Barr virus and who had an extreme sensitivity to electromagnetic radiation and chemicals. The caller had engaged the services of "an environmental specialist" who had buried metal "neutralizers" over several veins that he had located by dowsing and that were underflowing the house—all at considerable cost. No remission from the very painful condition had taken place, and after a reasonable time the "expert" had been asked to remove the devices. The caller requested immediate help, the response to which included the type of mental imprint already mentioned. A month later another call came. This time the voice was strong and vibrant: "He came to get his coils. He dowsed and dowsed, but *he couldn't find the veins where he'd buried them*. He was completely baffled. He went away empty-handed."

The third anecdote concerns a most courageous professional woman of 35, who wrote of her battle with atypical rheumatoid arthritis for 17 years. Pain, swelling, sores were her daily lot. The treatment of 22 October, 1988, involved no less than 56 geopathogenic zones that she habitually encountered, or had encountered, and which were still active in her subconscious.

(There were other considerations as well, of course.) All of these water flows were dealt with in the same way I've described—briefly and with mental imprint. On 13 March, 1989, the woman wrote of her recovery, stating, "I have been living with pain and discomfort for seventeen years and now I can brush my teeth or turn a door knob without wincing, stand up and be able to walk, and best of all to sleep pretty soundly. . . . I stopped taking medication. . . . It's a miracle!"

Does the fact that her rheumatologist could find no *visible* improvement, but agreed the medication should be stopped until further notice, suggest that, in addition to judgment by result, we need a whole new system of instrumentation and measurement in order to document and eventually understand the mystery of geopathogenic zones? Will this, in turn, require new concepts of mind and matter? A new cosmology? If we build the record, the explanation will come.

TERRY ROSS'S COLUMN,
THE CANADIAN DOWSER, FALL 1988

When dowsers ask, if they ask at all, why the rods react in their hands, do they settle for the explanation of "involuntary muscular movement"? Would you say it's a shibboleth—that is, an accepted view, a given—that the pendulum does its thing because the dowser's neuromuscular complex tells it to? Or is there another interpretation?

Chris Bird's book *The Divining Hand* contains a discussion of the ideas of the 19th century chemist Michel-Eugéne Chevreul, who found after two decades of intermittent study that he could enter into a particular state or disposition which he felt contributed to the actions of the pendulum. "Chevreul," Chris wrote, "came within a hair's breadth of anticipating twentieth century experiments that have proved the ability of peculiarly gifted individuals to cause movement in stationary pendulums and other motionless objects at a distance. . . . Other experimenters, however, were to come to conclusions that had narrowly escaped Chevreul. One of them, a French civil servant, de Briche,

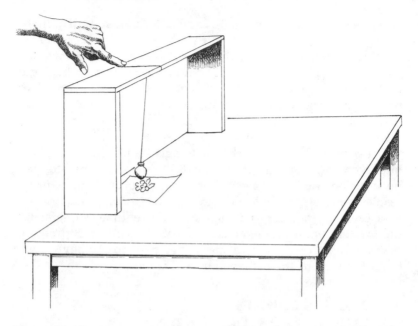

Figure 19. The apparatus used by de Briche, which showed that the experimenter could move the pendulum merely by touching the string and sending the intent that the pendulum respond in a specific manner.

tied the thread of a pendulum around a wooden support (Figure 19). He touched only that part of the thread that lay against the top of the support. Though he could not have imparted any movement to the hanging bob with his hand, it nevertheless produced oscillations that varied depending upon what substance lay beneath it."

Switch now to the brass desk lamp with the green glass shade that illuminates the page on which this is being written. Place your hand with mine on the top of the shade. The 5-inch pull chain suspended from the lamp beneath it—and totally insulated from it—will begin to rotate, either clockwise or counterclockwise, according to your will and intent. If you prefer, simply lean on the desk with both hands on the blotter. You'll obtain similar results. Do these reactions constitute evidence of "odic forces," as the Austrian chemist and inventor Baron von Reichenbach said it did, a force emitting from both the inert object and the animate being? Or of orgone, vril, bions, or prana?

None of the above, in this dowser's opinion! It reflects, rather, the structure of our subtle anatomy. There is an invisible organ—quite dowsable and known to dowsers since the days of pioneer ASD dowser Verne Cameron—that extends from the midbrow and acts like a "receiver" and a "transmitter." It creates a tiny (but measurable-by-dowsing) standing wave at its tip as soon as the dowsing question is asked. This wave resonates with the wave-form of the target whether the latter is near, beyond the horizon, solid, or intangible, for such "signature" waves exist for everything that is. That they exist on a level where time and space are fluid does not in any way make them less real; and that they can be brought into phase with the wave formed by the dowser's question accounts for the harmonic reaction of the device, and for the entrainment of the chain on my brass lamp, which just obliged me by its movement and signaled to me that this was so, without any physical contact whatsoever.

Therapeutic touch, dowsing, psychokinesis—perhaps they are all the same phenomenon.

Appendix F

Selected Bibliography

We offer the following list of books with a combination of enthusiasm and frustration: enthusiasm because each of them has, in different ways, enlarged our respective views of the world of dowsing, and frustration because we could list scores of books that have also done so to some extent or that are of historical interest for the dedicated student or that investigate areas of dowsing not of direct concern to this book. Many topics are grist for the dowsing mill, but those topics included in the books below should guide you as you begin the refining process.

The American Dowser. Danville, VT. Quarterly journal.

A source for the very latest information pertaining to dowsing world-wide. Its contents range from scholarly studies to informal anecdotal experiences. The journal is sent to all members of ASD and to various researchers and scholarly organizations around the world.

Bird, Christopher, *The Divining Hand*. New York, E. P. Dutton, 1979.

A beautifully illustrated, popular history of dowsing over the last 400 years, with documented accounts of modern dowsers. A good historical source book, although its stress is on explanations and experimentation related to conventional science. It does not cover the most recent research into consciousness or speculate on dowsing as a reach of the mind.

Bohm, David, *Wholeness and the Implicate Order*. London, Routledge & Kegan Paul, 1980.

The author's own account, written for the thoughtful layman, of the theory of the implicate order. A basic book for the scientific background of the new-age paradigm that we develop in this book.

Graves, Tom, *The Diviner's Handbook*. Rochester, VT, Destiny Books, 1990.

Another approach, more traditional, to the how-to of dowsing, written in a compact, orderly, easy-to-understand style, which touches lightly upon several of its applications without investigating the how or the why behind it. Graves is a well-known British dowser.

Hitching, Francis, *Dowsing: The Psi Connection*. Garden City, Anchor Press, 1978. (Out of print.)

Covers dowsing from earliest times, from historical record and inference, through modern "experiments" undertaken by the author in America and England. The approach is journalistic. Hitching is also the author of *Earth Magic* (New York, William Morrow and Company, 1977, out of print), which investigates megalithic man and his monuments, a topic of interest to many dowsers.

Howells, Harvey, *Dowsing For Everyone: Adventures and Instruction in the Art of Modern Dowsing*. Brattleboro, VT, Stephen Greene Press, 1979.

A chatty, highly anecdotal tour through the world of dowsing. Like any good tour, it covers the ground and creates enthusiasm. Don't look for any real depth, but this is a book you would give to a friend who is casually interested in dowsing.

Lonegren, Sig, *Spiritual Dowsing*. Glastonbury, Gothic Image Publications, 1986.

Sig organized the ASD Earth Mysteries group and wrote an Earth Mysteries handbook, available from ASD. This book presents his approach to learning the basics and dowsing earth energies.

MacLean, Gordon, *A Field Guide to Dowsing*. Danville, VT, American Society of Dowsers, 1976.

A concise and lively booklet written by one of the "grand old men" of dowsing, this gives the how-to basics of dowsing in the dry, compact manner of a Down-East Yankee. It was reprinted by popular demand.

Tansley, David, *The Raiment of Light: A Study of the Human Aura*. London, Routledge & Kegan Paul, 1984.

Covers the whole field of vital forces, the subtle bodies, and their critical role in physical and psychological health. It is recommended for those who feel ready to go further into the paradigm of man as composed of varying densities of light.

Wilber, Ken, Ed., *The Holographic Paradigm and Other Paradoxes: Exploring the Leading Edge of Science*. Boulder, CO, Shambhala, 1982.

A compilation of articles, appraisals, and commentaries on David Bohm's holographic theory. Authors include Karl Pribram, Renee Weber, Ken Dychtwald, Fritjof Capra, Kenneth Pelletier, Itzhak Bentov. It gives a good overview of Bohm's theory and its relation to many fields.

Willey, Raymond C., *Modern Dowsing*. Sedona, AZ, Esoteric Publications, 1975.

A painstaking account of the mechanics of dowsing, the various devices, and alternative ways to use them, both for on-site and map dowsing. Although mechanistic and now somewhat outdated, it is an early "standard" handbook, written by an engineer and charter member of ASD.